ORTHO'S® All About

Decorative Painting

Meredith® Books
Des Moines, Iowa

Ortho® Books
An imprint of Meredith® Books

All About Decorative Painting
Editor: Larry Johnston
Contributing Writer: Jeff Abugel
Senior Associate Design Director: Tom Wegner
Assistant Editor: Harijs Priekulis
Copy Chief: Terri Fredrickson
Editorial Operations Manager: Karen Schirm
Managers, Book Production: Pam Kvitne, Marjorie J. Schenkelberg
Contributing Copy Editor: Steve Hallam
Contributing Proofreaders: Dan Degen, Beth Lastine, Pam Wright
Indexer: Barbara L. Klein
Electronic Production Coordinator: Paula Forest
Editorial and Design Assistant: Kathleen Stevens

Additional Editorial Contributions from Art Rep Services
Director: Chip Nadeau
Designer: lk Design
Illustrator: Dave Brandon

Meredith® Books
Editor in Chief: James D. Blume
Design Director: Matt Strelecki
Managing Editor: Gregory H. Kayko
Executive Editor, Gardening and Home Improvement: Benjamin W. Allen
Executive Editor, Home Improvement: Larry Erickson

Director, Sales, Special Markets: Rita McMullen
Director, Sales, Premiums: Michael A. Peterson
Director, Sales, Retail: Tom Wierzbicki
Director, Book Marketing: Brad Elmitt
Director, Operations: George A. Susral
Director, Production: Douglas M. Johnston

Meredith Publishing Group
President, Publishing Group: Stephen M. Lacy

Meredith Corporation
Chairman and Chief Executive Officer: William T. Kerr

Chairman of the Executive Committee: E.T. Meredith III

Thanks to
Susan Goans Driggers, decorative painter, designfaux.com, for painting samples and providing instructions.

Photographers
(Photographers credited may retain copyright © to the listed photographs.)
L = Left, R = Right, C = Center, B = Bottom, T = Top
Ross Chapple: 7BR, 12CL, 30, 39
Stephen Cridland: 15C
DeGennaro Associates: 11BR
Tim Fields: 10B, 14BL
D. Randolph Foulds: 7BL, 20B
Ed Gohlich: 12TR, 25T, 51B
Barb Gordon: 22C
Jim Hedrich: 17T
John Hetherington: 23C, 36T, 36B
Hetherington Photography: 20T, 21B, 24B, 25C, 26T, 28, 29T, 29CL, 60T, 62, 77, 90, 92T, front cover
Bill Holt: 14TR
William Hopkins Sr.: 6B, 7T, 13BR, 17B, 18, 19T, 19B, 60B, 22B, 23T, 23BL, 50T, 51TL, 54T, 66B
InsideOut Studios: 27, 43, 44, 45T, 45BR, 46, 47, 48, 49, 52, 53, 55, 56L, 57, 58, 59, 61, 63, 67, 68, 69, 70BL, 70BR, 71, 72, 73, 74, 75, 76, 78, 79, 80, 81, 82, 83, 84, 85, 86, 87, 88, 89, 91, 92BL, 92 BR
Mike Jensen: 5T, 15B
Jenifer Jordan: 13T
Pete Krumhardt: 16
Jeff McNamara: 5B, 10T
Tom McWilliam: 14BR
Tommy Miyasaki/DeGennaro Associates: 4
Robert Perron: 15T
Richard Sexton: 32
Perry Struse: 6T, 21T, 25B, 26B, 29CR, 45BL, 50B, 51TR, 54B, 64, 65, 66T, 70T
Steve Struse: 23BR
Brian Whitney: 11BL
Marilyn Wynn: 56BR

All of us at Ortho® Books are dedicated to providing you with the information and ideas you need to enhance your home and garden. We welcome your comments and suggestions about this book. Write to us at:
Meredith Corporation
Ortho Books
1716 Locust St.
Des Moines, IA 50309–3023

If you would like to purchase any of our home improvement, gardening, cooking, crafts, or home decorating and design books, check wherever quality books are sold. Or visit us at: meredithbooks.com

If you would like more information on other Ortho products, call 800-225-2883 or visit us at: www.ortho.com

Library of Congress Control Number: 2001132252
ISBN: 0-89721-469-2

DECORATIVE PAINTING AND FAUX FINISHING

IN THIS SECTION

Decorative painting offers unlimited possibilities for customizing and personalizing your home. With brushes, paint, and a few readily available tools, you can change a bland wooden fireplace surround into a striking centerpiece that resembles marble. You can give an entire room the look of expensive custom-patterned wallpaper, or you can build subtle visual textures that seem to change with different light. On a smaller scale, decorative painting can make a plain dresser or table into a distinctive piece of furniture.

This book will show you how to apply those decorative painting and faux finishing techniques.

A faux finish—faux is the French word for fake—is a surface painted to look like something else, such as marble, wood grain, or stone. Decorative painting is a broader term that includes techniques that give surfaces a more distinctive look than ordinary painting. Decorative painting can be just a simple stripe along the edge of a tabletop or it can be an elaborate marbled mantelpiece.

You can achieve nearly any effect imaginable with the right paint and the right tools. The proven techniques in this book will show you how to create fabulous faux finishes. And you don't have to worry about mistakes: If you don't like the finish you've put on, paint over it with a base coat and start over.

Bold painted stripes and a grid make the walls points of interest in this room. Graphic designs like this require careful layout but aren't difficult to paint.

Simple stenciled designs on the cabinet doors combine with the marbled countertop and backsplashes to bring a distinct style to this kitchen.

Paint makes this room a showplace. The wood grain on the paneling and ceiling of this room isn't real—it's a faux finish. And the pattern on the wall above the paneling isn't wallpaper—it's decorative stenciling.

THE ART OF FINISHING

Faux wood grain against dark green paint enriches this table. Limiting the use of graining draws attention to it. (See page 66 for graining instructions.)

A painting technique, not time, crackled the paint on top of this table. (See page 56 for crackling instructions.)

A RICH HISTORY

Decorative painting has been done for thousands of years. Ancient Greek and Roman temples, now aged to pristine white, were usually gloriously, and often garishly, painted both inside and out.

In the early 19th century artisans created tools and special paint formulas to make less expensive surfaces, such as wood or plaster, look like real marble or stone. This ability to mimic nature with paint also led to the technique known as trompe l'oeil, which translates to "fool the eye." A wall painted to look like a large window with a view of a mountain range or ocean shoreline is an example of trompe l'oeil. That kind of work is beyond the scope of this book.

In time, decorative painting became highly esteemed in interior design. Faux-painted pieces were appreciated not merely because they looked like some other material, but as works of art in their own right. Schools of decorative painting were founded in Europe, and the art of faux finishing became a specialized art form with its own exotic and expensive tools and brushes. Graduates of these schools were masters of the techniques and were well rewarded for their skills.

FAUX REVIVAL

In the last few decades, these painting techniques have been demystified; millions of people have dressed up walls and furniture with paint. Manufacturers have developed new brushes, combs, tools, paints, and varnishes to make decorative painting easier and more effective. Numerous self-contained kits have appeared on the market, offering all you need for marbling, graining, or stenciling small pieces. Results offered by these kits can vary.

The basic, proven techniques shown in this book will help you create decorative painted finishes on a single wall, in whole rooms, or on pieces of furniture. These techniques use materials you can buy at any paint or crafts store or home center.

Combing adds both color and texture to this wall. Combing, like many other decorative painting techniques, helps to hide imperfections in the surface. (See page 54 for combing instructions.)

The green squares in this checkerboard pattern were stamped onto the wall with a sponge.

Faux marble is a versatile finish, suitable for furniture as well as for large surfaces such as the baseboard and wall panel in this entry. (See page 72 for marbling instructions.)

COLOR

Color comes from light. The science of light and color relates to a band of wavelengths in the broad spectrum of electromagnetic radiation. The band, called visible light, contains all colors. When a beam of light passes through a prism, the rays bend at different angles and fan out into a spectrum that runs from red through orange, yellow, green, and blue to violet.

Color is more art than science to most people. Color is how we see the world—it is one of the ways we recognize and classify things around us and it often expresses emotion or sets a mood. Color also is one of the most affordable ways you can change your surroundings at home.

Effective design begins with color. It can set a room's personality, define its style, establish its mood, and alter its apparent size. Color can also accent a room's advantages, hide its faults, and turn an otherwise dull space into a warm, inviting one. One color alone usually can't achieve these changes; several colors are needed to complement and reinforce a particular look or mood. This selection of colors becomes your color scheme for decorating (see page 16).

COLOR WHEEL

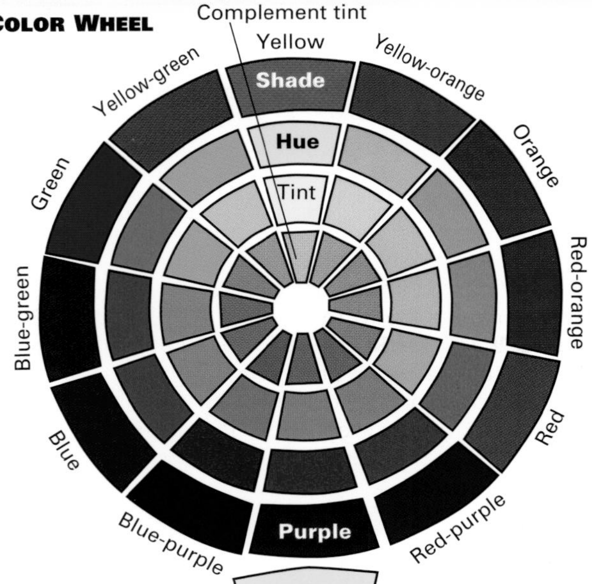

EXPANDING THE WHEEL

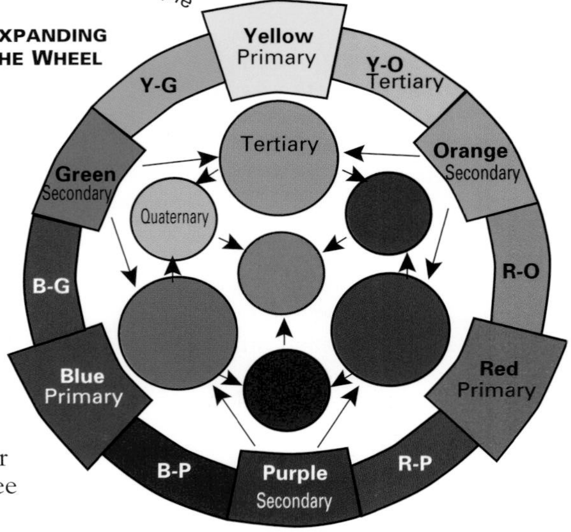

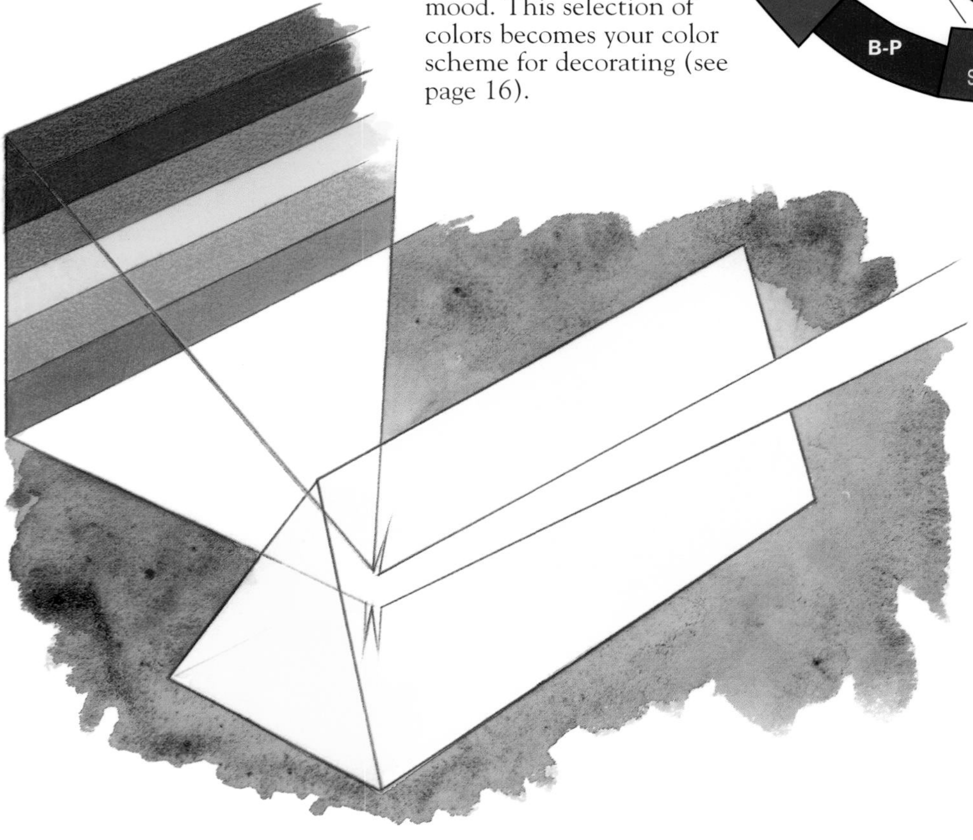

THE COLOR WHEEL

Interior designers rely on knowledge of the color wheel, above left, to help determine colors for a decorating scheme. Understanding the relationships between colors and how they influence each other to create different looks will help you create pleasing color schemes. Colors fall into three categories:

PRIMARY COLORS: Primary colors are the three pure colors in sunlight—red, yellow, and blue. They are the first level of color; primaries are the basis for creating all other colors and cannot be broken down into other colors. Primary colors are at equal distances around the color wheel.

SECONDARY COLORS: The second level of colors includes orange, green, and purple. They are called secondary colors because each is created from equal amounts of its two adjacent primary colors. On the color wheel, each secondary color falls halfway between the two primary colors it contains, and is directly opposite the third.

TERTIARY COLORS: The third level of colors includes those created by mixing two secondary colors or a secondary color and a primary color, in any proportion. Purple and orange, for example, combine to make a terra-cotta color.

COMBINING COLORS

The color wheel helps you to determine which colors work well together. There are no rigid rules about how colors should be used together, but there are natural combinations that are always successful and look pleasing. The following combinations are standards. They are the easiest combinations for beginning amateur decorators with modest experience to use to create a harmonizing color scheme.

ANALOGOUS COLORS: Any three colors located next to each other on the color wheel are analogous. Yellow-orange, yellow, and yellow-green make an analogous arrangement. So do blue-green, blue, and blue-purple. These are harmonizing plans because the colors are closely related; your eyes easily pass over them.

COMPLEMENTARY COLORS: These are colors opposite each other on the color wheel. The best example is the red and green of Christmas. Another is peach and turquoise. By combining exact opposites, this type of color combination balances warm and cool colors. Complements stimulate one another, but can seem garish when intense colors are used. Paints of complementary colors mixed together in equal amounts make a flat, dull, gray color.

TRIAD COLORS: Three colors spaced equidistantly from each other—such as red, blue, and yellow—make a triad. This is a complex, lively color scheme, so controlling color values and intensities is important.

SPLIT COMPLEMENTARY: This scheme combines a color with the color on each side of its complement. Red with blue-green and yellow-green makes a split complementary scheme. This subtle shift in the complementary colors enriches the scheme. These combinations require a little more planning to be effective.

DOUBLE SPLIT COMPLEMENTARY: This combination uses four colors, one from each side of two complementary colors. This is a rich color scheme, but difficult to do well.

MONOCHROMATIC: In this scheme, one color is used in many values and intensities so the mix stays lively and interesting. This is a sophisticated scheme that needs texture contrasts to work well.

NEUTRAL: This plan employs whites, grays, and black to build an elegant color palette. Some designers include browns—ranging from cream to chocolate—in this category. The neutral scheme requires value, intensity, and texture contrasts to be effective.

To use most of these formulas at their best advantage requires a range of values and intensities. For instance, in the classic Christmas colors, the red is a pure and intense hue but the green is a deeper shade than the pure green, darker in value and lower in intensity.

COLOR COMBINATIONS

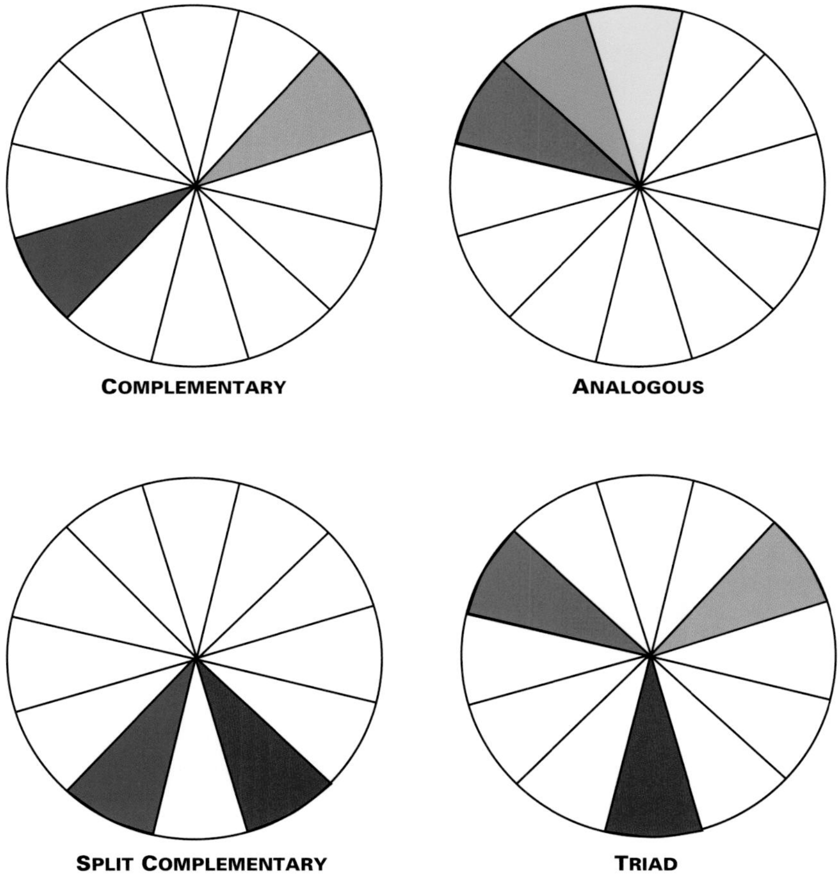

COLOR CHARACTERISTICS

Pure colors are seldom used in interior design. Pure red would probably overpower most rooms, for instance, but a darker or lighter red might be vibrant and warm. Modifying the characteristics of a color can increase subtlety and soften the color's impact, giving you a wider range of colors to choose from. Colors can be modified by mixing primary or secondary colors with one another or with white, black, or gray in different proportions.

Stippling on this wall reduces the intensity or value of the color. Many decorative paint techniques soften a color this way.

Intense hues like the red, yellow, and blue in this room create a bright, lively atmosphere.

HUE, INTENSITY, AND VALUE

Every color has three characteristics: hue, intensity, and value.

HUE, the most basic characteristic, is simply another word for color. Red is a hue.

INTENSITY, also called chroma, is a color's degree of purity, or saturation. Think of intensity as describing a color's brightness or dullness. A color appears more vivid and intense to the eye when it contains more true color, or hue. Adding its complementary color or black to any color reduces its intensity. The more you add, the grayer and duller the color becomes. Differences in intensity provide contrast between colors.

VALUE refers to the lightness or darkness of a color. As a color is mixed with white or black, it moves away from its pure hue, becoming a tint or a shade.

VALUE SCALE

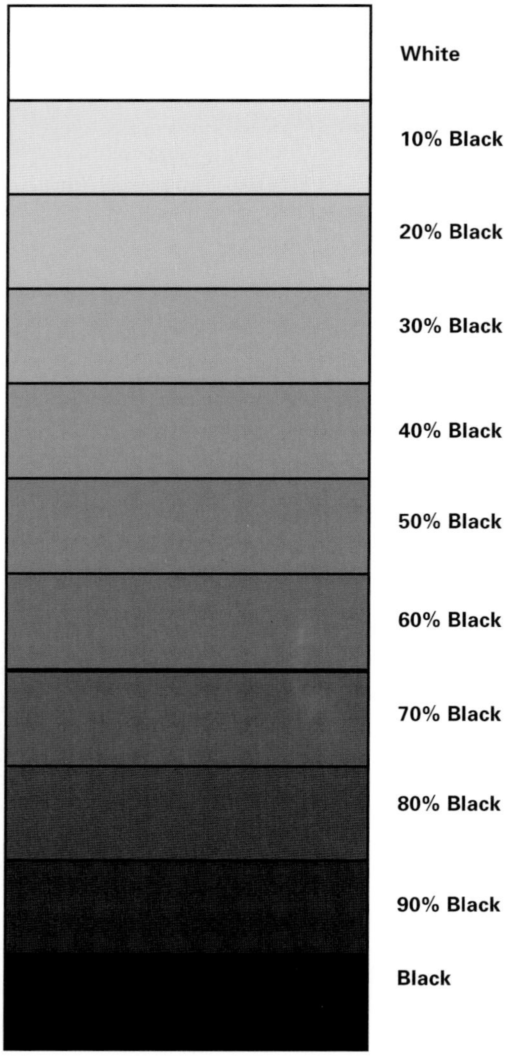

A tint is a hue that has been lightened by adding white. The more white added, the more pale the color. Pink is a tint of red.

A shade is a color that has been darkened by adding black to it. The more black, the darker the color. Maroon is a shade of red.

Mixing a color with gray gives a tone of the color. Cranberry is a tone of red.

White, black, and gray—white and black mixed together—are neutral. Theoretically, white and black are not colors. They either reflect all the colors in the visible spectrum (white) or absorb all of them (black). Adding neutrals to a color scheme introduces highlights and shadows, and enhances dimension.

VALUE SCALE

Color values introduce variety into a color scheme. The value scale extends from white at one end to black at the other. In between are graduated shades of gray—usually shown in 10 steps for convenience. The shades of gray represent the relative lightness or darkness of a color, somewhat similar to the way colors appear in a black and white photograph. Pure yellow has a higher value—it's lighter—than pure blue, for instance. But, some shades of yellow have the same values as tints of blue.

All colors that relate to the same level on the scale have the same value. Bringing different values of different colors into your decorating scheme will help control contrast.

For instance, blue and green don't always work well together, but a high-value pastel blue and a low-value dark green can be pleasing together.

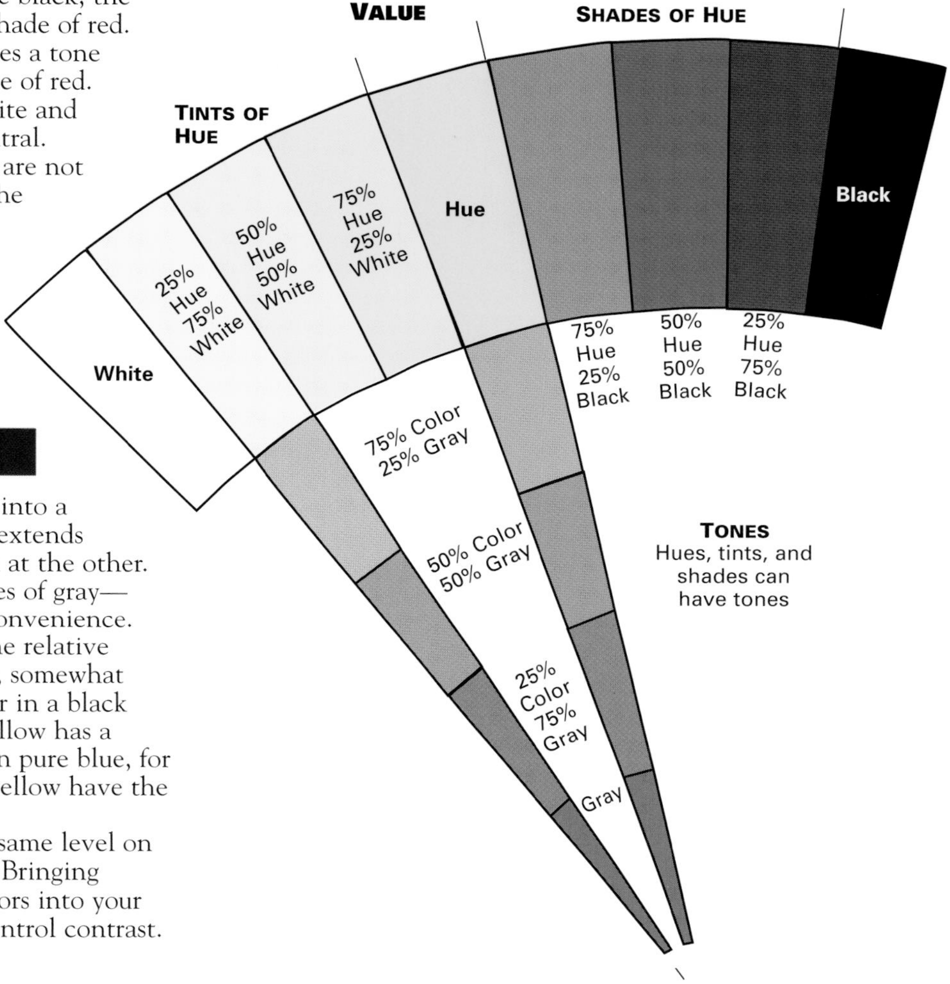

Color values of the green stripes at left are closer together than the values of the dark blue and white stripes at right. The strong contrast between the blue and white stripes makes them look brash and bold. The green stripes contrast less, so they are more subtle.

COLORS WITH FEELINGS

Color often describes emotion. Red is identified with anger, green with envy, blue with sadness. Optimists view the world through rose-colored glasses. And, of course, there's purple passion. Research has shown that colors do stimulate emotional and physical reactions in people, so each color has a psychological value that must be considered when planning your color scheme. Each color must feel right to you as well as look right.

Green and blue color-washed walls bring the colors of the sky and the lush foliage outside the window into this relaxing room. (See page 50 for instructions about color washing.)

Melon-color paint adds a rosy warm glow to this living room.

RED

Red is warm, bold, stirring, and energetic. In its pure form, it can increase a viewer's heart rate and raise body temperature. Use red in rooms where activity occurs, like a family room; one where sleeping and resting is not a priority. For a deep, intense setting, use other colors sparingly in a red room. The eye is drawn to red, so it makes an effective accent color.

YELLOW AND ORANGE

Yellow and orange are just as exciting as red, but more cheerful than festive, more bright than stimulating. Yellow and orange can warm and enliven any room. They brighten spaces especially well and can create an illusion of light in a dark room. Lighter values work best when applied to large surfaces.

GREEN

Green is the dominant color in nature. It is pleasing, cool, fresh, calming, even restful to most people. Green is a good color for any room where you want a calm and relaxed—but fresh—atmosphere.

BLUE

Blue, the color of sky and water, makes you feel fresh, cool, and restful. Blue walls make a south- or west-facing room seem cooler. Because blue recedes visually, it also lends the illusion of space and distance and feelings of haughtiness, formality, reserve, and sadness. In spite of these contradictory feelings, blue is a favorite because it is so easy on the eyes and the nerves. Blue is an excellent choice for rooms where you want to relax or sleep.

PURPLE

Purple makes most people think of lushness, regality, and passion. It is an intense and highly emotional color, partly because it straddles the line between the warm red and cool blue. This makes it a difficult color to use in interior design; it is usually used most effectively as an accent.

BLACK AND WHITE

Black and white are pure contrasts: light and nonlight, all and nothing. Both dramatic and elegant, they can lend an air of refinement and urbanity to a decorating scheme.

PUTTING COLORS TOGETHER

Designers have an eye for color—how colors combine with each other and how they work together. Most designers learn this skill—they are not born with it. You can develop the same expert eye by studying how color is used around you.

Perhaps the best way to study color is to clip pictures of rooms that you like and keep them in a file. Add new clippings and color swatches as you find them. Go through them occasionally and weed out the ones that don't appeal to you anymore. Over time, you'll be able to see your preferences in the colors and combinations of colors you are consistently drawn to.

Nature is a good place to start when developing a color scheme. Look at the colors in the brilliant plumage of birds or a dramatic seashore sunset. Color combinations found in nature please most people and are easy to recreate in your own environment.

Look at paintings and tapestries in museums and galleries. Art is an excellent source of inspiration, but the paintings of the Impressionists—Manet, Monet, Degas, Renoir, and others—are especially helpful because they show how colors placed side by side merge visually to create another color when seen from a distance.

Read decorating magazines. The articles are excellent resources because the homes shown are usually created by professional interior designers. Advertising in these magazines can be a great source of inspiration too.

Look at Oriental rugs as well as drapery and upholstery fabrics. Study the countless wallpaper books available at wallcovering stores. Take some books home to see the colors in your house. Ask your paint dealer for pamphlets and color chips that show the color combinations available.

Browse high-quality furniture showrooms. The displays are arranged by interior designers to emphasize effective color schemes in order to sell the store's total design services. Model homes and decorator showhomes are other useful sources of ideas.

As you look at room designs, notice the hues, values, and intensities used, and the proportions between them. Try to relate what you see to the color wheel, and note the combinations you find pleasing.

Take into account the colors you like—those that make you feel good. Notice which colors dominate your wardrobe and what colors you are most often wearing when people compliment you on your appearance. The colors that make you look your best are ideal colors for your home. Don't pick colors that make your family look sallow or flushed.

Deep purple walls look dramatic in this traditional living room. Brown kraft paper was torn and pasted to the walls before painting to create the textured surface.

Color fads come and go. When trendsetting designers start using certain colors, other designers and manufacturers often follow, making everything from bath towels to picture frames in these trendy hues. After a while, the colors become so commonplace that what once seemed new and exciting looks trite and ordinary. Then the cycle starts over with a new color fad.

You can use these color trends to your advantage in decorating; featuring currently fashionable colors can give your home a contemporary look. To keep your colors current, you will have to redecorate periodically.

If you want to redecorate less frequently, choose colors you like and can live with for a while, whether or not they are currently in style. Combine them in thoughtful color schemes for a look that you can live with and enjoy for a long time.

Black and white combine to make elegant-looking marbled squares. (See page 72 for instructions about marbling.)

LIGHT AND COLOR

When you're choosing colors for your room, look at your paint samples in the room itself. Lighting changes the way we see color, so paint samples will look different with the store lighting than in your home. Each type of room light shows color differently. Sunlight, which contains the wavelengths of all colors, shows the truest color. Fluorescent lighting often makes a color look greener, but some fluorescent tubes give more natural light. Incandescent lighting often strengthens reds.

How the room is lighted affects color. General room lighting may light walls and ceilings fairly evenly. Whether the light is natural, incandescent, or fluorescent will affect the color. Task lighting directs intense light to a specific work area—usually a surface—but may leave walls unlit, making dark walls look even darker. Accent lighting adds visual interest to a room, often by washing over walls or ceilings. Task lighting and accent lighting may be either fluorescent or incandescent.

Lights concealed behind a molding illuminate the wall and ceiling in this room and a floor lamp lights the lower part of the wall.

An accent light shining up from behind the potted tree washes the wall and eliminates a dark corner.

Ceiling-mounted track fixtures create pools of light for artwork hanging on deep red walls in this entry hall.

POINTERS ABOUT USING COLOR

Here are some techniques to help you use color with confidence. Limit the number of decorative techniques, colors, and paint effects in a room—too many reduces the impact and interest of them all.

■ Pick a key color for your home and use it in some way in each room. It can be the dominant color in one room, the secondary color in another, an accent in the third, the color of an accessory in a fourth, and so on. This technique will create color harmony throughout the house.

■ For color coordination, tint white ceiling paint slightly with the base-coat color used for the paint technique in a room.

■ Strive for balance in shades and tints of warm colors. A room decorated solely with pale tints can look weak and dull, while one painted entirely with dark shades will probably seem gloomy. A color scheme composed only of midtones can be monotonous. Variety is the key to a dynamic and refreshing look in a room.

■ Light colors are expansive and airy; they make rooms appear larger and brighter. Dark colors are sophisticated and warm; they make large rooms appear intimate.

■ Offset bright, bold colors—or many different colors—in a room by painting the woodwork and ceiling white. The white offers visual relief from the intense colors and gives the eye a place to rest.

■ When using different hues or paint techniques in several rooms, paint spaces between the rooms, such as hallways, with neutral colors to avoid clashes.

■ If you want dark or intensely colored walls, seal them with a coat of clear polyurethane after painting to enhance their depth and reflect the light. This is especially important if the room is small or dark.

■ Neutral paint colors that blend with neutral walls, ceiling, and floor will hide surface flaws. Most decorative painting techniques help cover blemishes too.

■ To make a room seem taller, carry the wall color up to the ceiling line. If there is a crown or cove molding, paint it the same color as the walls. Painting the ceiling a light color also makes it seem higher.

■ To visually reduce ceiling height or make a room feel cozy, stop the wall color 9 to 12 inches below the ceiling, then paint the band the same color as the ceiling. You can also paint the ceiling a dark color without the band of color at the top of the walls.

■ Make a long, narrow room seem wider by painting the short walls a darker color than the long ones.

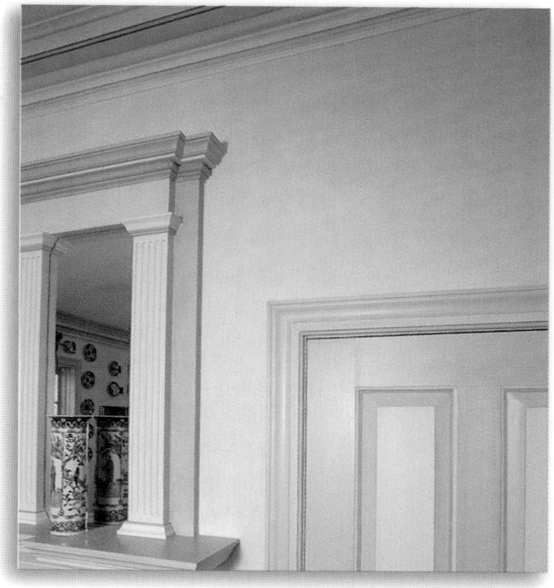

Polychrome decorating—the use of many colors—was popular during the Victorian Era. It is effective in rooms like this with complex moldings and woodwork.

A wide border made of heavy embossed wallpaper painted to match the ceiling visually lowers the ceiling to give this bedroom a cozy atmosphere.

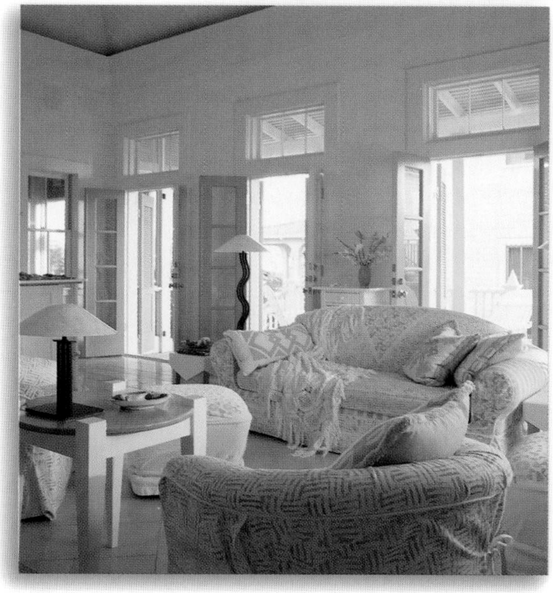

Pink and blue walls and ceiling make this room look like a cool and airy tropical refuge. Deeper colors in the fabrics and accessories keep the room from looking bland.

DEVELOPING A COLOR SCHEME

Moss green is the dominant color for these walls. Combing below the chair rail has the effect of adding a lighter tint of the same color.

An effective color scheme usually combines no more than three colors, plus a neutral. Don't add more colors, especially when you will be applying decorative effects that often incorporate two or more colors themselves. Instead, use variations in value and intensity to create contrast between colors. The color wheel will help you choose colors that work well together. Although the colors you consider will seldom be the pure hues found on the color wheel, you can visualize where they would fall on the color wheel.

DETERMINING THE AMOUNT OF COLOR TO USE

Incorporating your selected colors in the right proportion is the most important part of a color scheme. It's also the most difficult. In fact, because few people feel confident with creating a color scheme, they tend to use a favorite color over and over until it loses its impact. Avoid this common mistake by employing one of the following methods to create your color scheme.

ONE COLOR DOMINANT: Use one color in its different values and intensities over most of the room. Then use complementary, analogous, triad, or split-complementary colors as accents on smaller furniture pieces, window coverings, accent rugs, and accessories such as pillows.

A monochromatic arrangement is another version of this design plan. It also employs one color in shades and tints of different values. This scheme uses only one accent color—a contrast to the base color that is often its complement.

SPLIT COLORS: Use one color on the walls, the window coverings, and most upholstered furniture; a different color on the floor; and a third color and variations of the first two for accent furniture and accessories. This is an excellent way to use a triad or split-complementary color combination. Just be sure you get significant contrast in the colors' values and intensities.

TWO DOMINANT COLORS: Use one dominant color for the walls, floor, and smaller pieces of furniture, and another color for the major pieces of furniture. Because you use only two colors, you must pay special attention to the mix of contrasting values and intensities. You must also add texture contrasts to the total scheme. The textures can be in the paint or wallcovering or in the upholstery and accessory fabrics.

COLORS ON WALLS

Walls are the most obvious places to begin designing a color scheme. They constitute the largest surface in a room, and the way you finish them affects everything else you do. Yet that doesn't mean they have to dominate your decorating scheme: The walls can provide the background for a decorating scheme or they can become its focal point.

BACKGROUND WALLS: Choose the color for walls that will serve as a backdrop after selecting the other major decorating elements. This lets you find a color with a balance of hue, value, and intensity to complement all the colors in the room. It's much the same way the matting around a picture emphasizes its colors. Modern techniques for matching and mixing custom colors make it easy to match paint to the colors in a carpet or fabric. However, it may be difficult to find carpet or fabric that matches a paint color. Decorative painting techniques should be subtle in color and pattern for background walls.

The wall color can be a shade or tint of the room's dominant color; a shade or tint from a pattern in the room's carpet, decorative fabrics, or wallcovering; or a shade or tint that's in another item in the room.

The wall color can also be a shade or tint of a color that complements the dominant color. You probably will find that complement used in one of the patterned fabrics in the room. This is the best way to choose a new color for the walls in a room where nothing else will be changed.

A neutral color makes the walls a true backdrop, because they will not call attention to themselves. A subtle decorative technique—such as combing or sponging—can make the walls more appealing without making them stand out brashly.

FOCAL-POINT WALLS: If the walls or one wall will be the most important feature in the room as well as the largest, choose the wall finish first and build your color scheme around it. This is more difficult than picking a background color because, like an artist starting with a clean canvas, you have to decide what you are going to do without referring to anything else in the room.

The easiest way to choose a color for a dominant wall is to make a selection based on your favorite colors. You also can select a particular decorative painting technique—such as graining—for one wall, then base the color for the rest of the room on that. Another way is to decide what mood you want a room to convey. Consider a room's function, decorative style, size, natural light, and exterior weather conditions; then make your color choice. Your selection should focus mainly on whether the room should be light or dark, warm or cool. If the room receives little light, the wall color should be light—unless, of course, you want the room to be dark and cozy. Whatever wall finish you choose, make sure its color, texture, and pattern suit the room's style and use.

Any architectural problems in the room should influence your decision on a color where the walls are the focal point. Color, texture, and pattern all affect what the room looks like and how you feel in it.

Light colors, subtle textures, and small patterns usually make a room seem larger and taller. They are ideal choices when you want the room to seem larger than it is or when you want to emphasize the spaciousness of a room. If the ceiling is too low, consider a strong vertical pattern, such as stripes. Dark or intense colors, bold and coarse textures, and large or busy patterns make a room seem smaller because they bring the walls close to you. That can be an advantage in a room that is too large or where you want a cozy, intimate effect. It can also emphasize the comfort of a small room.

You can either hide or highlight woodwork or other architectural features. To make them recede, paint them a color that matches the wall; to make them stand out, paint them a distinctive hue or a contrasting value.

Stippled and sponged walls serve as a background for art objects in this room.

Sponge-stamped diamonds make the wall itself a decorating element.

TOOLS AND MATERIALS

IN THIS SECTION

Tools and materials for creating faux finishes and decorative paint effects come from two different worlds: wall painting and art.

Paints for decorative painting and faux finishing fall into two broad categories—standard interior wall paints and artist's paints. Which one you use for a particular project depends largely on the technique you'll be working with and the scale of the project—whether you are painting a stationery box for your desk, the desk itself, or the walls of your home office.

Tools include ordinary paintbrushes and rollers, along with artist's brushes and some special tools developed for specific techniques. Some tools are as simple as rags and sponges.

Here's a look at the paint, tools, and other materials you'll use for decorative painting and faux finishing.

This special brush leaves a linenlike texture in the paint, which is first applied with a roller. Most decorative painting techniques use special tools with common paints.

Parts of Paint

Whatever kind of paint you use—artist's paint or wall paint—is available as either an oil- or water-base material. All paints are made of four standard ingredients: solvent, binder, pigment, and additives.

Solvent (sometimes called the paint vehicle) is the liquid base of the paint. This component makes up the majority of the mixture. Water is the solvent for latex paints; a petrochemical solvent (alkyd is common) is the vehicle for oil-base paints.

Binder holds the mixture together, helps it adhere to surfaces, and gives the surface a distinctive sheen, such as gloss or matte.

Pigment is a finely ground powder that gives paint its color.

Additives are mixed into paint for a variety of purposes, ranging from reducing mildew to enhancing durability. Wall paints are more likely than artist's paints to contain additives.

Standard latex interior paint crackles when spread over crackle medium. This is a simple, two-coat, decorative finish.

Many decorative paint techniques and faux finishes, such as the graining shown here, call for translucent glazes.

WALL PAINTS

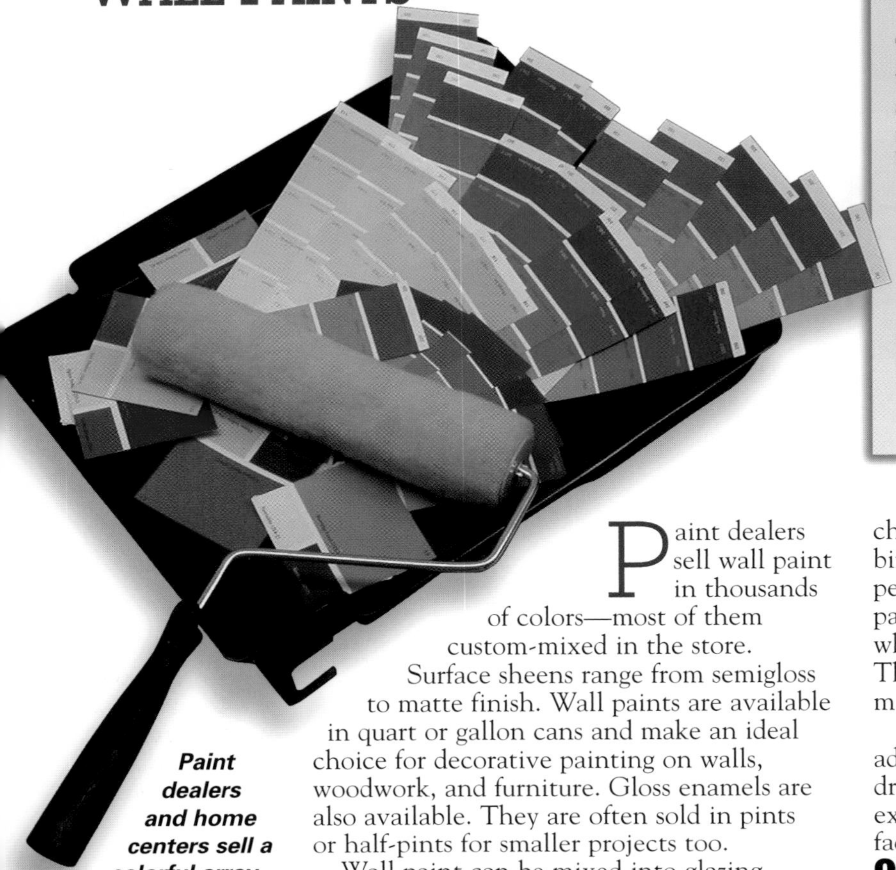

Paint dealers and home centers sell a colorful array of wall paints.

DON'T MIX OIL AND WATER

The key to avoiding problems with painted walls and projects is to remember that oil and water don't mix. When gathering materials for the finishes described in this book, remember that oil-base enamels, artist's oils, and alkyd paints can be mixed together on the same surface and can be thinned with turpentine or mineral spirits. Likewise, artist's acrylic color and latex paints can be mixed and thinned with water. Some finishes look best with oil-base products; others are just as easy to achieve with water-base paints.

Paint dealers sell wall paint in thousands of colors—most of them custom-mixed in the store. Surface sheens range from semigloss to matte finish. Wall paints are available in quart or gallon cans and make an ideal choice for decorative painting on walls, woodwork, and furniture. Gloss enamels are also available. They are often sold in pints or half-pints for smaller projects too.

Wall paint can be mixed into glazing medium (a colorless base) to make a translucent color tint which is used to create special effects.

LATEX PAINT: Most of the paint sold is latex, a water-base paint that dries quickly and cleans up with water. It is nonflammable, nearly odor-free, offers superior color retention, and resists chalking. It's the best choice for painting walls and furniture. The binder in a high-quality latex paint is 100 percent acrylic resin; in a low-quality latex paint, the binder is 100 percent vinyl resin, which decreases the durability of the paint. The plasticity of latex paint's coating can make sanding between coats more difficult.

A top-quality latex paint gives excellent adhesion over wood and wall surfaces such as drywall, plaster, and masonry. Latex paints are extremely resistant to sun bleaching and fading compared to oil-base paints.

OIL-BASE PAINT: Oil-base paint—also called alkyd paint—was once the standard material for all painting. Both pros and do-it-yourselfers now prefer latex paints for their ease of application, low odor, and simple water cleanup. Oil-base paint requires paint thinner for cleanup. It tends to sag and run during application and dries slowly. Today, oil-base paint is mostly used for interior doors and trim or to paint directly over existing oil-base paint.

These sponge-stamped green squares were done with standard latex wall paint. Latex interior paints are economical and easy to use for many decorative effects on walls, floors, ceilings, woodwork, and furniture.

ARTIST'S PAINTS

Artist's paints—either oil or acrylic—come in small containers and are ideal for wood-graining a small item like this box.

Sold by art-supply dealers or crafts stores, artist's paints are formulated for fine-art painting—creating something that might hang on a wall rather than putting a fresh coat of color on the wall itself.

Artist's paint, also called artist's color, is heavier-bodied than wall paint—it's almost like toothpaste and usually comes in a similar type of tube. Artist's paint gives more intense color than most wall paint. Both oil- and water-base materials are available. The range of colors available in artist's paints is narrower than the selection of hues for wall paints. Many artist's colors take their names from pigments used by painters centuries ago—burnt umber, cobalt blue, and cadmium yellow, for example. Many of these pigments were expensive, unstable, or toxic. Synthetic pigments produce the same colors more economically and safely.

OIL PAINT: While oil paints are the time-honored standard for works of fine art, there are plenty of alternatives today that dry faster and are easier to use for faux finishes. You can thin artist's oil paints with mineral spirits, and you can tint or shade them with other oil colors or powder pigment. But oil paint takes a long time to dry, unless you add an accelerator. Brushes for oil-base paints should be made with either natural bristles or synthetic bristles that won't be affected by oil-paint solvents. Art- or craft-supply dealers can help you select the correct brushes to use with oil paints. Cleanup requires thinner or turpentine. Oil-base formulas have been used for centuries to create finishes similar to those shown in this book, but water-base artist's paints—originally developed to give artists a simpler alternative to oil paints—work wonders for painting faux finishes as well.

ACRYLIC PAINT: This fast-drying, water-base paint is manufactured as a thick formulation packaged in tubes or as a liquid packaged in small bottles. Widely available, acrylic paint can be used for painting on anything from canvas to kitchen cabinets. It's used for painting decorative designs on walls and furniture or for stenciling and stamping. It's also a great substitute for latex wall paint when you're working with smaller areas or adding touches of color to a glaze. It dries quickly, but additives like glazes or extending mediums will slow the drying, so you have more open time for working. You can thin acrylic with water or acrylic medium. Acrylics are available in standard artist's colors as well as a wider range of hues. Some acrylics produce special effects, such as pearl colors or metallics. Apply acrylics with synthetic-bristle brushes. Plastic tools and containers are better than metal ones when working with acrylics; they won't rust.

Artist's paints and crafts paints are available in several forms and a wide range of colors.

OTHER MEDIA

Heavy-bodied stencil paint is pounced onto the surface with the end of a stiff brush.

Tinted glaze adds color to a surface but isn't opaque like paint. Glaze is used in many decorative painting techniques and faux finishes.

Crackle medium, applied over a base coat, will crackle any paint applied over it. On this table, red will show through the crazing in the antique white top coat. The result is a finish like the one shown bottom left on the opposite page.

GLAZE: A neutral-color translucent base, glaze is at the heart of many faux finishes. Available in oil- or water-base varieties, glazes are colored by mixing varying amounts of paint color into them—oil color for oil-base glazes, acrylic or latex for water-base glazes. The glaze is then applied to a base-coated surface and results in a translucent appearance. Ragging, combing, sponging, or other effects are then created with the appropriate tool. Glazes extend a paint's drying time, making it easier to create the final effects you want.

STENCIL PAINT: This heavy-bodied paint, available as either oil- or water-base material, is applied by dabbing with a stiff-bristled stencil brush. Because it is less fluid than other paints, it is less likely to creep under the edges of the stencil.

STAIN: Unlike opaque paint, stain is a translucent finish. On wood, stain imparts color while allowing the grain to show through. Stains are generally available in two types: pigmented stains and dye stains.

Pigmented stains are similar to thinned paint. The pigment can build up in open grain, accentuating it. Pigmented stain is usually sold premixed in liquid or gel form and ready to apply. It comes in a variety of natural wood tones, or you can custom-color the stain using glazing medium and paint.

Dye stain, often called aniline dye, penetrates the wood, often giving clearer color. Dye stain, available in wood tones and other colors, is generally sold as a powder which must be dissolved in water, alcohol, or another solvent (depending on the powder) before use. Water-soluble dye stains are usually considered the most fade-resistant, but they raise the wood grain, which requires additional sanding for application.

Stains can be brushed on, wiped on with rags, or sprayed on, depending on the surface and the desired effect.

CRACKLE MEDIUM: Paint on wood cracks and crazes after long periods of time. Some cracking occurs as the wood expands and contracts with humidity changes; some is due to weather effects and light. To simulate aged, cracked paint, a wide variety of crackle products is available. Some crackle finishes are brushed over paint, some are painted on between coats of paint, and some are applied from spray cans. In all cases, you should follow the manufacturer's preparation and application instructions for best results.

VARNISH: Acrylic varnish is a water-base sealant that is ideal for water-base paints and finishes. Quick drying and durable, acrylic varnish comes in matte or semigloss.

Polyurethane varnish is used over water- or oil-base paints and stains and provides a tough, durable finish. Polyurethane is available in gloss, semigloss, or matte finishes.

Varnish frequently adds an amber coloration to a finish, so it's a good idea to apply some to a test piece to see what the final effect will be.

Spray varnishes are nonyellowing and are available in matte or gloss finishes. They provide much lighter protection than the brushed-on varnish sold in cans, however.

SHELLAC: Shellac is good for sealing and aging gilded and bronzed surfaces and is often used to seal stencil paper. The thinner for shellac is alcohol.

WAX: Wax offers another way to seal finishes on wood, though it doesn't hold up well when it is the sole finish for surfaces that are subjected to wear. Furniture wax and floor wax are readily available and work well on small projects. Wax provides a soft, deep sheen that lends the luster and feel of age to many pieces. Follow the manufacturer's instructions for applying and buffing wax.

High-gloss polyurethane varnish will protect the graining on this panel and add depth to its appearance.

Aniline dye comes as a powder. Stirring about 1/8 teaspoon of the water-soluble powder into 4 ounces of hot water makes a brilliant, transparent dye.

Paint applied over crackle medium cracks as it dries. The base color shows through.

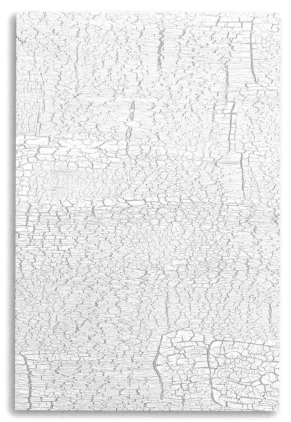

Paste wax gives a soft sheen and some protection to painted surfaces on furniture and small objects.

PRIMERS AND SEALERS

Primer-sealers made for wall painting will prepare surfaces for decorative finishes.

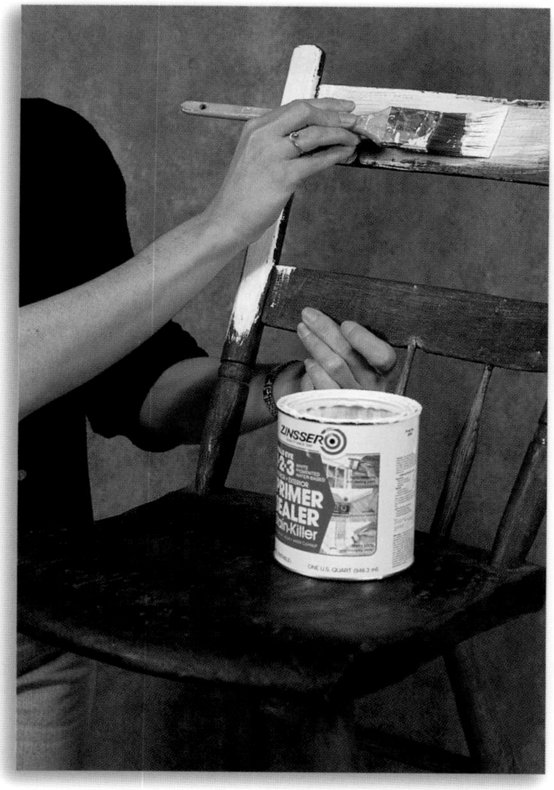

White-pigmented primer-sealer will hide the old, dark finish on this chair and prevent stains from bleeding through the new decorative paint.

Primers and sealers cover old finishes and seal the surface after you've lightly sanded it or prepared it for painting. Primers and sealers go on before the base coat is applied. You may need to use a primer-sealer, or a blocker (a densely pigmented primer) when a light paint will be applied over a dark or intense color. Knots in wood are particularly stubborn and often show through even several coats of primer—so use a blocker. If you're going to stain the surface or color-wash it, don't use primers because they will block your efforts. Also, don't apply primer if you are going to distress the surface (see page 58) because the primer itself will show through. Match the primer to the type of paint you are using (oil- or water-base). You can have it tinted to match your base paint color so fewer base coats are needed for good coverage.

A primer or sealer applied to the surface before painting will improve the appearance and durability of the finish.

SEALER, also called undercoater, includes products such as white-pigmented sealers, oil-base undercoats, and sanding sealers. On a porous surface, sealer prevents absorption and

Primer-sealer will cover the tired old finish on this frame so an attractive new decorative finish can be applied. Clean and sand the old finish first so the primer-sealer will adhere.

Spray application is often easier for items like this frame. A spray handle (available from paint dealers and home centers) snaps onto an aerosol can to minimize hand fatigue.

uneven appearance of later coats. Sealer is often applied to isolate surface problems—such as discoloration, knots in wood, or mildew—to keep them from marring the finished surface.

Some sealers, such as KILZ, are available in spray cans that offer good coverage and easy application. An inexpensive trigger handle (see above right) makes the spray can easier to control and eliminates painted fingers and hand cramps.

PRIMER provides a uniform base color and texture and helps top coats adhere better. Primers are usually acrylic water-base products; they dry faster than paint.

WHEN TO USE A SEALER

APPLY A SEALER TO THESE SURFACES:

- Bare open-grained woods such as oak and maple
- Bare woods, such as redwood or cedar, that are likely to bleed through or discolor paint
- Large areas of wallboard joint compound or patching plaster
- Masonry surfaces such as unglazed brick, cinder block, and concrete
- Metal surfaces; apply an oil-base primer-sealer with rust inhibitors to prevent corrosion
- Any unpainted surface before painting, including new plaster, new drywall, and old woodwork that has been stripped

The smooth, even coat of primer-sealer makes base-coating and finishing the frame easier.

WHEN TO USE A PRIMER

APPLY PRIMER TO THESE SURFACES:

- Any surface that has large sections repaired with joint compound or patching plaster
- Existing paint that is sound, but thin or worn
- Over dark or bright colors that you want to cover with lighter paint.

BRUSHES

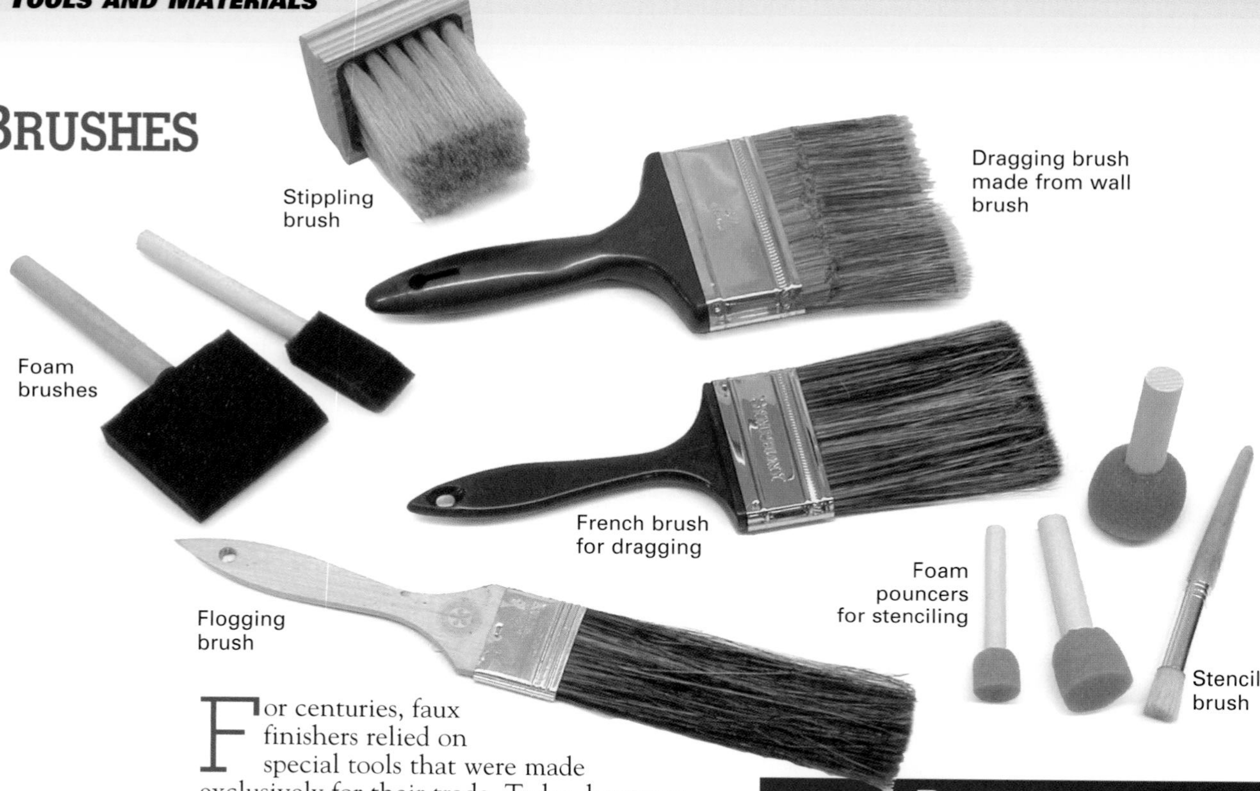

For centuries, faux finishers relied on special tools that were made exclusively for their trade. Today, however, everything you need is readily available. While it's tempting to look for bargains, it's best not to skimp on brushes. Their quality will have a lot to do with the appearance of the final finishes you achieve.

BASE-COATING BRUSHES

Brushes intended for general painting are the ones you'll use to apply primers or base coats, fill in patches of color, and spread varnish or other protective top coats over the completed job. A 3-inch sash brush—an angled brush designed for painting trim and molding—is a good choice for base-coating anything from furniture to walls. Sponge or foam brushes in 1- through 3-inch widths are fine for applying base coats. They are inexpensive enough to discard after use. Wide artist's brushes, when retired from fine detail work, also make great base coat brushes. Beware of brushes with stiff bristles; they will leave marks in the paint.

Artist's brushes

ARTIST'S BRUSHES

Designs are painted with artist's brushes that come in flats, rounds, and liners. For acrylic paints, synthetic fiber brushes work well. When working with oil paint, red sable brushes are preferred. Brush styles, like flats and rounds, look just as their names suggest. Liners are for fine line work, and fan brushes feature broad spread bristles to fan out paint for special effects.

BRUSHES FOR DECORATIVE FINISHES

These brushes are essential for creating special painted effects. Ordinary house painting brushes are fine for base coating and experimenting, but many decorative effects and faux finishes can be done properly only with specialty brushes. Here are some of the brushes you'll probably need:

STENCIL BRUSH: This round bristle brush has a short handle for the quick, dabbing

LOADING THE BRUSH

Your approach to the simple task of dipping a brush into a can of paint may not matter much when painting a wall one color. But how you put the paint on different types of brushes can make a big difference for decorative painting. For example, some techniques call for double-loading, which means carrying two colors on a brush side by side, with a smooth blend between. Side-loading means carrying one color on just one side of the brush. Various strokes—like comma strokes and S or U strokes—are used when painting roses, vines, or other artistic decorations. Where instructions for a painting technique call for loading the brush in a special way, practice loading the brush and making the stroke on a piece of scrap material before you start your project.

hand movement stenciling requires. Stencil brushes are available in many sizes, so choose the one that best fits the design area.

FRENCH BRUSH: This small flat brush with short bristles is used for stippling and some brushed textures.

STIPPLING BRUSH: Made specifically to help create the subtle, deep, all-over texture of a stippled surface, this is a flat-ended bristle brush without a handle.

DRAGGING BRUSH: This wide brush with short, soft bristles is used to create the look of woven fabric and similar textures and to blend colors.

CARING FOR YOUR BRUSH

Your project will be easier if you have the right brushes and specialty tools for decorative painting; you'll also get better results, especially if you buy the best. You should keep the brushes in top condition.

Whether you are using water-base paints or oil-base paints, avoid letting a brush stand on its bristles in a container of water or thinner for any length of time. This distorts the bristles and damages the brush. It's better to clean the brush immediately after you've finished working. Clean the brush every two hours or so during use too.

■ When using or cleaning a brush, always work the bristles in their natural direction.

■ Rinse your brushes often. This keeps paint from drying in the bristles, which is sure to shorten the life of a brush. Clean paint off the metal ferrule as well.

Professional painters often use the same brushes for years because they know how to care for them. To get maximum service from your brushes, condition new china bristle brushes by spraying the bristles with a small amount of WD-40 or 3-in-1 oil. Soak synthetic-bristle brushes for latex paints or acrylics in liquid fabric softener for a day, then rinse with water. These simple conditioning steps make cleanup easier and prolong bristle life. If you use your brushes frequently, recondition them occasionally.

■ Clean brushes at the end of the job or the end of the day. When dry, store each brush in its original cover or in a cardboard cover. To make a cover, measure and cut cardboard to fit around the brush, allowing the edges to overlap. Tape the edges together and slide the brush inside. Hang your brush by the handle.

When you're ready to retire a brush, don't throw it out. Worn brushes are great for some painting techniques, like stippling and creating textures. They also are handy for preparation work, such as dusting or sweeping out corners.

CLEANING BRUSHES

CLEANING A BRUSH—LATEX PAINT: Here's how to clean a brush used for latex or acrylic paint:

1. Scrape off excess paint against the edge of a 5-in-1 tool.

2. Mix a gallon of warm water with ½ cup of fabric softener in a 5-gallon bucket. Dip your brush into the mixture, swish briskly through the water, and count to 10. Your brush will be completely clean when you remove it from the water. Clean other tools in the same manner.

3. To fast-dry your paint brush, use a paint brush spinner to spin water from the brush. (Or spin the handle between the palms of your hands; see below.) Spin the brush in an empty bucket.

CLEANING A BRUSH—OIL-BASE PAINT: To clean a brush used for oil-base paints, follow these steps:

1. Scrape off excess paint against the edge of a 5-in-1 tool.

2. Number-label three clean glass jars, such as mayonnaise jars. Fill jar 1 about two-thirds full with mineral spirits. Put a 50–50 mixture of mineral spirits and denatured alcohol in jar 2. Put denatured alcohol in jar 3.

3. Dip the brush into jar 1, then spin the excess out into an empty bucket.

4. Dip the brush into jar 2 to dissolve remaining paint, then spin again.

5. Dip the brush in jar 3 for a final cleaning, then spin dry.

6. Finish by swishing the brush in a liquid fabric softener mixture as described in Step 2 of cleaning a latex-paint brush.

To spin the brush, whirl the handle between the palms of your hands.

ROLLERS AND PADS

Rollers and painting pads are often used for base coating. You can quickly paint a wall with a roller. A pad, with its small, flat surface, is best suited for cutting in—painting along corners or trim on the wall. A pad spatters and drips less than a roller, and can be used with either oil-base or water-base paint. Most pads come with their own paint tray and lid.

PAINT ROLLERS

A standard paint roller will quickly base-coat a wall or other large, flat area. Smaller rollers—both narrower and smaller in diameter—are handy for base-coating small items or for painting some special effects. A corner roller—a narrow sponge roller with beveled edges—is often useful for decorative painting.

When selecting a roller, make sure the handle is comfortable to grip and has a threaded socket in the end so you can add an extension pole. (Or buy a roller frame with a telescoping handle.) An extension handle, particularly an adjustable one, provides a fast, easy way to paint high on walls and on ceilings. A conventional roller cage should have a smooth cap at the end of the roller head to prevent marring adjacent walls.

ROLLER COVERS: A sponge roller is the best kind to use. It holds more paint than a conventional napped roller cover, and because the sponge doesn't have fibers or a nap, it won't splatter as much paint on you or leave fuzz on the wall.

Slip-on roller covers are made for either latex or oil-base paint. Use a latex-paint cover only for water-base material and an oil-base paint cover only for oil-base paint.

Napped roller covers must suit the surface and paint—shorter naps usually give a smoother finish. Embossed roller covers paint a repeating design on a surface, much like a rubber stamp.

ROLLER TRAY: If you use a metal roller tray, slide it inside a plastic trash bag, then press the bag into the pan to create a liner. The plastic makes it easier to clean the tray—simply turn the bag inside out and toss it in the trash. It also prevents water-base paint from rusting the metal tray, which contaminates the paint. You also can fold the plastic liner over the tray so it becomes a lid to keep the paint from drying during a break.

PAINT GRID: You can load your roller quickly, neatly, and evenly with a square plastic paint bucket with a built-in grid. You can also buy a separate plastic grid to hang in your own bucket.

CLEANING ROLLERS AND PADS

Clean rollers and pads the same way as described for brushes. Use the water-base cleaning method for water-base rollers and pads, and the oil-base method for oil-base rollers and pads.

Disposable roller covers are a good choice for some jobs. After the job, throw away the cover instead of cleaning it. To pull it off the frame, put your hand inside a plastic bag, grab the cover through the bag, pull it off, then fold the bag down over the cover for disposal. Clean the roller frame.

If you are stopping to take a break but will resume painting later, wrap the roller cover tightly with plastic food wrap instead of cleaning it. The wrap will keep the paint from drying on the roller.

OTHER HANDY ITEMS

COMB: Rubber combs for painting look a bit like hair combs. The teeth cut through glazes on surfaces to create patterns and textures.

SPONGES: Natural sea sponges are best for marbling and sponging textures onto surfaces. Cellulose sponges can be used for more subtle effects, as well as for applying stains. Cellulose sponges are also easier to cut into smaller pieces for stamping or stenciling designs.

Sponges

STENCIL MATERIAL: Precut designs on clear acetate or polyester sheets are readily available. But you can cut out your own using a crafts knife or heated stencil-cutting tool and stencil material. Stencil material and stencil-cutting tools are available from crafts stores. Use a stencil brush or sponge to dab on the paint.
FEATHERS: Available at art and crafts stores, long bird feathers are used to create veining and cracking effects in marbled surfaces.

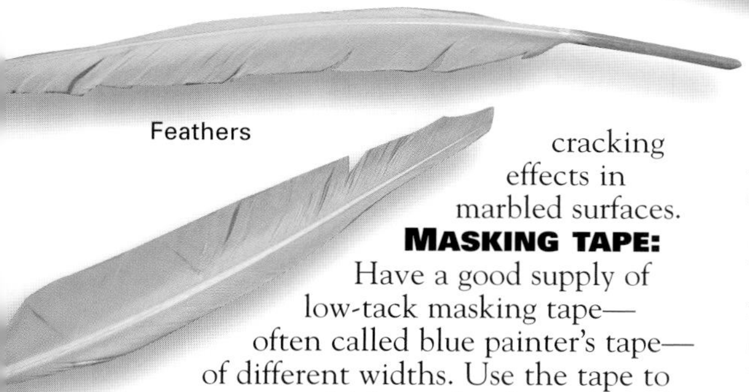

Feathers

MASKING TAPE: Have a good supply of low-tack masking tape—often called blue painter's tape—of different widths. Use the tape to cover areas which need to be protected when paint is applied. It also holds stencils in place and is used in laying out some paint designs. Striping tape—specially cut to make painting stripes easy—can also be found at many paint or crafts stores.
PAINTER'S PRETAPED MASKING FILM: This handy combination of blue masking tape and plastic sheeting creates an instant drop cloth with tape along one edge. It comes in a cartridge that fits into a holder with a cutting edge. The film protects the 24 inches from the wall where most accidents occur. The plastic clings to the surface and paint drops dry on it almost instantly. The sheeting is biodegradable too.
PLASTIC GLOVES: Wear plastic gloves; latex gloves are porous and allow the paints to come through. Wear a thin plastic glove inside a ragging glove. Before you put on plastic gloves, sprinkle a little cornstarch or baby powder on your hands to help keep them dry.
DROP CLOTHS: Protect the floor with a drop cloth when you're painting a piece of furniture or a wall. The best drop cloths have a heavy plastic side and a paper side. Lay the cloth with the paper side up. Never use newsprint for drop cloths because the black ink can mar clean surfaces. Bedsheets are too porous; the paint will pass right through.
TRISODIUM PHOSPHATE: Known as TSP, this agent washes dirt and grime from walls. Mix ¼ cup with a gallon of warm water to wash walls. Apply it to the walls with a mop, let it set for two or three minutes, then scrub the walls with Scotch-Brite. This wet sanding will keep dust in the water. Wear plastic gloves; TSP is caustic and can burn skin.
PAINT CLEANER: A water-soluble, citrus-base cleaner, such as Goof Off, removes paint from rugs, floors, and woodwork.
NONSTICK KITCHEN SPRAY: Kitchen vegetable spray will keep paint from sticking to your skin. Apply it to exposed skin before you start painting.
VINEGAR: Stir 1 cup of vinegar into 1 gallon of water to rinse walls after washing them with TSP.
PLASTIC FOOD WRAP: Clingy plastic food wrap protects anything that can't be removed from a room or a piece of furniture, including doorknobs and pulls. Wrap the telephone receiver to protect it from messy hands. Pull a sheet taut over the front of your glasses to keep spatters off the lenses.
CORNSTARCH OR BABY POWDER: Before putting on plastic or rubber gloves, sprinkle your hands with either of these to keep them from getting sweaty and wet.
BABY WIPES: These are good for easy cleanup. They are safer than oil-soaked rags that can spontaneously combust.

Combing tools

Graining tool

WHERE TO START?

IN THIS SECTION

When applying random, nonrepeating finishes to small, decorative items such as urns or vases, deciding where to start is simple: You can start virtually anywhere. The same is true for medium-size items like chairs, tables, or even fireplace mantels. Finishes can be applied (or wiped off if necessary) in a relatively short time with little effort. But that changes when you want to put a decorative finish on a wall or a whole room.

Finishing a single wall, or all the walls of a room, presents several challenges. You'll need more primer or base coating paint and a larger quantity of the paint ingredients for your finish. If the technique you're using requires artist's paints in tubes, buy an extra tube to ensure you won't run out before you're done. You'll have to protect the floor and furniture as if you're doing a standard paint job.

Base coats or primers can be applied with a brush or roller just like any other paint. As you're working on the layers that will create your final finish, extenders will give you more open time; the work won't dry while you're still working. But because you're working on a large area, you shouldn't stop in the middle of the wall and resume the work later. The new application will likely create a line against the old that can really mar the final appearance.

Unlike normal one- or two-coat paint jobs, decorative finishes like ragging, stippling, combing, marbling, and others often require several applications after the base coat is applied. Speed can be an important factor. So when painting rooms, divide each wall into areas that you can comfortably paint within the working time available. Start in either the left or right upper corner. Paint the sections consecutively, maintaining a wet edge to blend the sections together as you work your way across the wall. Stop for the day at corners or other natural breaks.

The diamond pattern of the trellis was laid out on this wall with masking tape before sponging on the finish and painting the grapevines. Centering the trellis pattern on the wall is crucial to the overall appearance, even though the vines and other elements are asymmetric.

PLANNING THE PROJECT

Glazed squares adorn the walls of this dry bar. The squares are centered on the wall and have been sized so the ones at the corners and edges are full size.

Painting decorative or faux finishes on a wall or around an entire room takes its toll on your arms and shoulders—and sometimes, your nerves. So if you're not sure you have the stamina and patience, plan to paint just a wall or two per session, rather than doing an entire room at one time.

Taking on too much can lead to smudging and overpainting on the adjacent wall in corners. The finish on adjacent walls should blend together to avoid an unsightly border. To avoid problems in corners, protect the wall you're moving toward with wide masking tape tucked into the corner. Let the paint dry on the first wall, then put masking tape on the corner of the wall you've finished and remove the tape from the unpainted wall. Then paint that wall, after applying tape to the corner of the next wall. Make sure the paint doesn't build up into a line of its own against the edge of the tape in the corners.

LAYING OUT THE JOB

Stripes and other painted finishes that create a distinct or repeating pattern look best centered in the room. To make sure the pattern will look right once you've painted it, lay out the job before you start.

FINDING THE FOCAL POINT

To begin the layout, stand in the doorway and look for the room's focal point. The focal point is probably on the vertical centerline of one of the following walls:

- The first wall you see as you enter the room. The centerline runs down its middle.
- The room's main window or windows (often located opposite the door). If there is only one window, no matter what its size, it is the focal point and the centerline runs through its center. If there are several windows, but they are on different walls, the larger window is the focal point. When two or more windows are close together or side by side, the centerline lies midway between them. Corner windows, or windows near the corner on two adjoining walls, make a focal corner. The centerline runs through either the largest window or the window closest to the corner.
- The wall above a fireplace.
- The largest exposed wall in a bathroom or kitchen.
- The main wall in a kitchen eating area.

The focal point of the room is at eye level on the vertical centerline of the focal wall you have identified. Mark the focal point at eye level with a No. 1 pencil. This becomes the starting point for planning a trial layout

FOCAL POINT OF A WALL

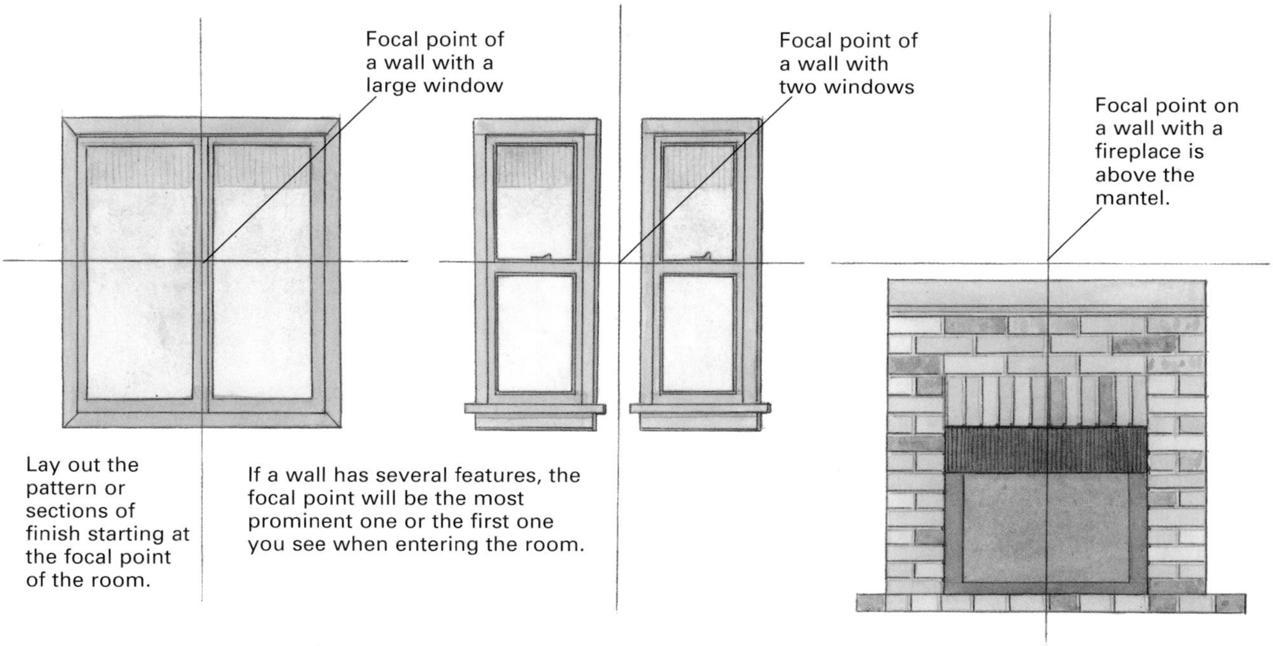

two windows

pattern or

finish starting at

If a wall has several features, the

prominent one or the first one
you see when entering the room.

of your pattern, but it is not the point where you will begin painting.

To lay out the pattern, start at the vertical centerline through the focal point. You can center the first pattern section on the centerline or make the centerline the edge of a section. Adjust the pattern width to fill the wall evenly. The pattern will then flow across the wall both ways from the focal point. If the pattern goes around a corner onto the next wall or goes around the entire room, you can adjust the pattern width on the end walls slightly to make it come out evenly at the corners again.

The most inconspicuous spot in the room—called the dead corner—is a good place to start painting. Common dead corners include corners behind doors, the header space above the entrance door, and hidden alcoves. Starting in one of these inconspicuous spots allows you to get comfortable and adept at painting the pattern before you come to the most visible parts of the room.

CENTERING THE DESIGN

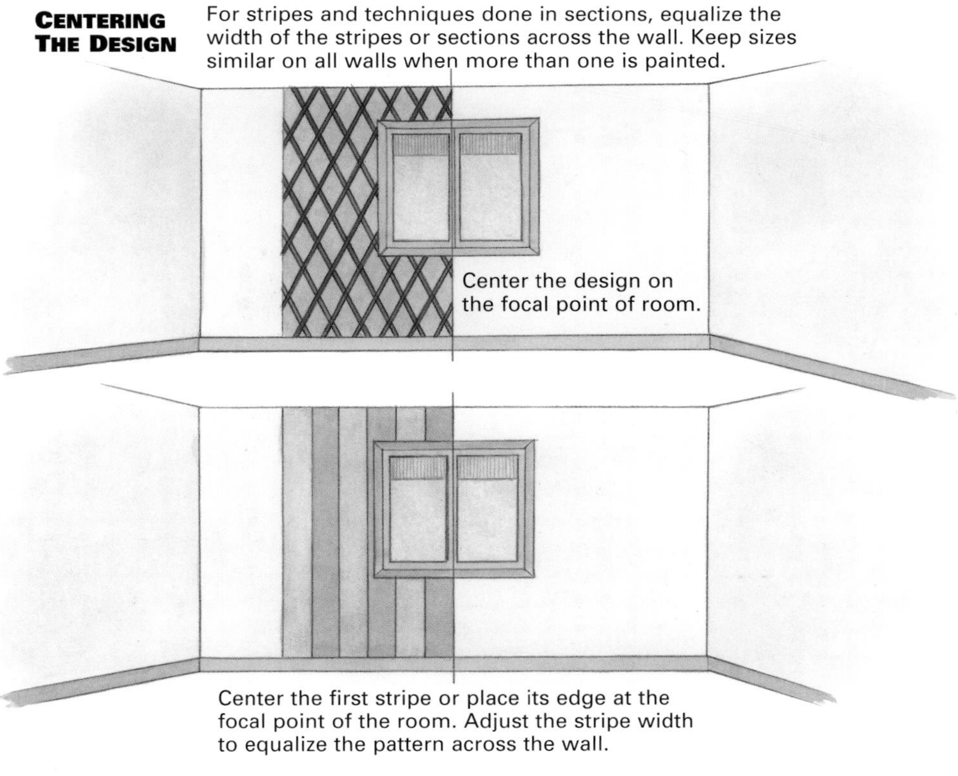

For stripes and techniques done in sections, equalize the
width of the stripes or sections across the wall. Keep sizes
similar on all walls when more than one is painted.
Center the design on
the focal point of room.
Center the first stripe or place its edge at the
focal point of the room. Adjust the stripe width
to equalize the pattern across the wall.

HOW MUCH PAINT DO YOU NEED?

ESTIMATING SURFACE AREA

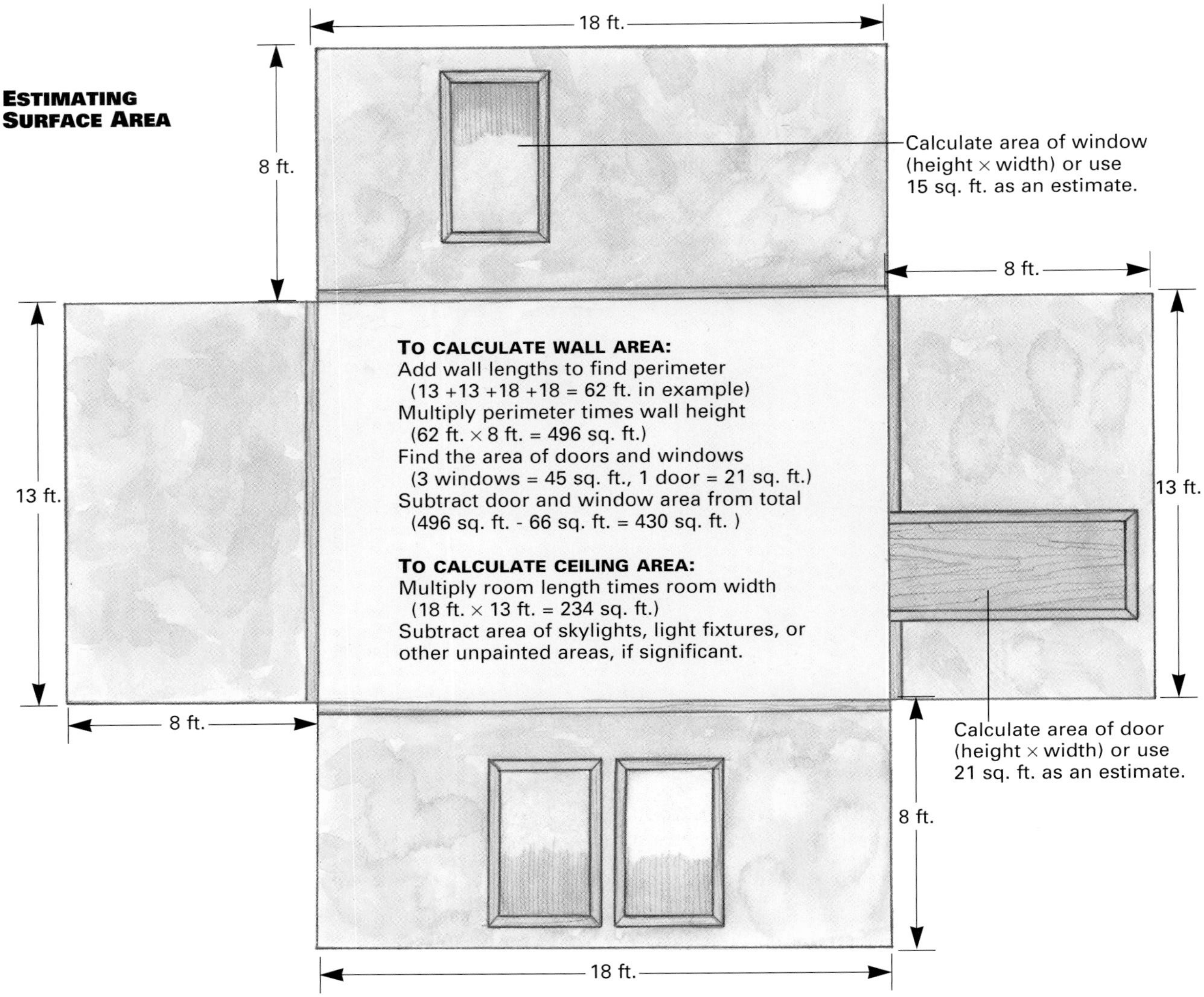

18 ft.
8 ft.
Calculate area of window (height × width) or use 15 sq. ft. as an estimate.
8 ft.
13 ft.
TO CALCULATE WALL AREA:
Add wall lengths to find perimeter (13 +13 +18 +18 = 62 ft. in example)
Multiply perimeter times wall height (62 ft. × 8 ft. = 496 sq. ft.)
Find the area of doors and windows (3 windows = 45 sq. ft., 1 door = 21 sq. ft.)
Subtract door and window area from total (496 sq. ft. - 66 sq. ft. = 430 sq. ft.)
TO CALCULATE CEILING AREA:
Multiply room length times room width (18 ft. × 13 ft. = 234 sq. ft.)
Subtract area of skylights, light fixtures, or other unpainted areas, if significant.
13 ft.
8 ft.
Calculate area of door (height × width) or use 21 sq. ft. as an estimate.
8 ft.
18 ft.

PURCHASING PAINT

- Although many paint manufacturers claim that one gallon of paint will cover 400 square feet, it's safer to estimate 300 square feet of coverage per gallon. Using this figure will keep you from running out of paint in the middle of a wall.
- Always buy slightly more paint than you need. This extra amount allows for spillage, waste, and spots that soak up more paint than expected. Plaster, for example, is more absorbent than wallboard. Also, you'll want some leftover paint for future touch-ups.
- Buy extra paint if you plan to paint the interiors of built-in bookshelves or cabinetry.
- Colors can vary slightly from batch to batch, so it's best to buy all the paint you're likely to need at one time instead of running out, then having to match the color. If your job calls for several gallons of custom-mixed paint, minimize color variations by mixing the cans together in a 5-gallon pail. Then pour the blended paint back into 1-gallon cans.

There's nothing more frustrating than realizing near the end of the job you don't have enough paint to complete it. And while it's good to have a little extra paint on hand for later touch-ups, it's a waste of money to be stuck with a lot of leftover paint. To avoid either situation, accurately estimate the amount of paint you will need. Here's how to do that:

1. Begin by calculating the square footage of the surfaces to be painted. Measure the length and width of the room to determine its perimeter—the distance all around the room. For example, if the room is 13 feet wide and 18 feet long, its perimeter is 62 feet (13 feet + 13 feet + 18 feet + 18 feet).

2. Multiply the perimeter by the height of the room to find the number of square feet of wall area. If the room is 8 feet tall, then the wall area is 496 square feet (62 feet × 8 feet).

3. Count the doors and windows in the room. Then subtract from your wall area 21 square feet for each standard door and 15 square feet for each standard window. If your room has large doors—such as a sliding patio door—or large windows, you can measure the width and height of each door and window, then figure the exact square footage of each. You don't need to be precise; round to the nearest square foot. The room in the example has one standard door and three standard windows, so subtract 66 square feet from the wall area (21 square feet + 3 × 15 square feet).

The net wall area to be painted is 430 square feet (496 square feet – 66 square feet).

4. To find the number of gallons of paint needed for one coat, divide the wall area by 300—the coverage in square feet for a gallon of interior paint. In the example, you would need a little over 1.4 gallons to paint the walls; round that up to 1½ gallons—1 gallon and 2 quarts—or even 2 gallons.

5. Consider your paint technique and how much of the wall area each color will cover. For a combed finish, for instance, you'll need enough of both the base color and the glaze or top color to cover the entire area.

EARTH-FRIENDLY PAINT

Paint once contained toxic elements such as lead, chromium, and mercury. Those have been removed from almost all consumer paints, and chlorofluorocarbons (CFCs) have been eliminated from aerosol paints. Manufacturers are working to reduce volatile organic compounds (VOCs) in paint, the remaining environmental concern.

VOCs include the petroleum-based solvents used with oil-base paints. They give the paint a spreadable consistency, improve its ability to accept color pigments, maintain a durable film, and help it dry to a level surface. Small amounts of solvent are used in latex paints.

VOC vapors escape into the atmosphere and become part of a complex chemical reaction that produces ozone, a component of smog. At the time the problem was identified, about 2 percent of the VOCs in the atmosphere came from paint.

Today, most latex paints contain no more than 10 percent solvent, and many contain only 4 to 7 percent. The solvent content of oil-base paints has dropped from 50 percent to about 20 percent.

Water-base latex paints have improved so much in the past few years that they have become the first choice for many professional painters. They have greater colorfastness, better adhesion, and allow the surface to breathe better. Simple water cleanup makes them easier to work with and reduces the use of solvents that could harm the environment.

LOOK OUT FOR LEAD

When you're preparing for a project, you could encounter old paint that contains lead. Paint that was applied as recently as 1978 could contain lead; the older the paint, the more likely it contains lead. Almost all paint once contained lead, but lead content declined with the development of latex paints from the 1950s until lead limits were set for all paints in 1978. Dust and chips from damaged or degraded lead paint can contaminate your house and cause serious health problems for you and your family. For safety, lead-bearing paint that's loose, chipped, or breaking down should be eliminated from homes. A simple swab test kit, available at paint and hardware stores, will confirm whether paint contains lead.

THE BEST WAYS TO ELIMINATE LEAD-PAINT HAZARDS IN A HOUSE INCLUDE:

■ **PAINT REMOVAL:** Scrape paint from peeling walls and woodwork with a broad knife. You can apply chemical paint strippers to soften the paint. If you dry-scrape the paint, mist the surface with a spray bottle as you work to reduce hazardous dust. Wear a respirator while you work. Clean up dust and particles with a wet mop—a vacuum cleaner will spread lead dust around.

Sanding, sandblasting, and similar methods aren't recommended because of the dust hazard. And softening lead paint with a heat gun could create toxic fumes.

■ **ENCAPSULATION:** Instead of removing the paint, isolate it or seal it off. Apply new drywall over the existing wall or float the wall with wallboard compound.

■ **SURFACE REPLACEMENT:** Remove woodwork and moldings painted with lead paint and replace them with new pieces.

PREPARING FOR PAINTING

Making the surface right for decorative finishes will prevent problems while you work and will make the finished project look better.

An easy-to-handle random-orbit palm sander saves time and effort when preparing surfaces for painting.

CLEANING WALLS

Before you begin painting walls, wash off the greasy film that forms on all walls. Dust the surfaces with a vacuum cleaner or sweep them with a clean broom or dust mop. Then wash the walls with a low-phosphate multipurpose household cleaner mixed according to the manufacturer's instructions. To make your own solution, combine a gallon of warm water with ½ cup trisodium phosphate (TSP) or a substitute in a 5-gallon bucket. Mix well.

Using a sponge mop with a scrubbing head, dampen the wall from the bottom up, working around the room. When you reach the starting point, turn the mop head around and scrub the wall. This is called wet sanding. If you plan to paint the ceiling, wash it first. Change the solution often to keep it clean.

For rinsing, mix 1 cup of white vinegar in a gallon of lukewarm water. The astringent vinegar neutralizes phosphors that might prevent the paint or wallpaper from bonding correctly to the wall. Apply the rinse to the wall with a clean sponge mop, using a fresh gallon of the rinse for each wall.

SANDING

In most cases, light dry sanding will be enough to prepare a surface. (If you have holes or cracks to patch in the wall, do that first, then sand to ensure a smooth surface.) A wallboard sanding screen, a hand sanding block, or a power sander will do the job. A random-orbit palm sander or half-sheet sander will do the best job of power-sanding; belt sanders are too aggressive for painting preparation. Sand walls along the longest direction; sand wood with the grain.

Walls coated with a flat or semigloss paint that has been wet sanded with a low-phosphate cleaner do not need to be dry sanded. Lightly sand high-gloss paints with 150-grit sandpaper. Wipe off sanding dust with a clean, damp sponge and change the sandpaper frequently. Wear a respirator, and close off the room to keep dust from spreading. A box fan placed in the window, front side facing out, will blow fine dust out of the room.

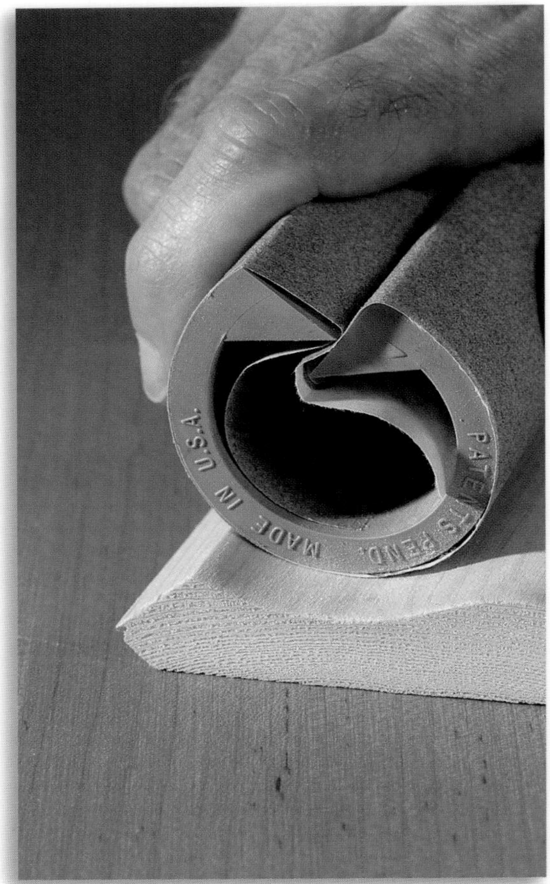

Hand-sanding with a flexible sanding block is the best way to smooth curved surfaces.

MAKING SURFACES READY

Here's how to prepare surfaces for decorative paint or faux finishes:

WOOD: New wood needs to be sealed and primed. A light sanding with 100-150 grit sandpaper will give you better adhesion and a smoother finish. Wood that has old paint can be sanded too, or stripped completely, depending on how rough the surface looks.

Paint stripping is usually messy; do it outside to avoid fumes and possible fire hazards. Once the paint is off the surface, remove all traces of the paint remover. Unlike metal surfaces that you can spray-wash with water, wood should be kept away from water completely, so prepare the surface with hand-sanding. Primer-sealer makes a great base for a painted finish, but it should not be used if you will stain the wood. The wood grain should show through stain, instead of being blocked out by paint.

PLASTER: Old plaster walls provide a good base for faux finishes and decorative painting. Patch cracks or damaged areas as shown above. Secure loose plaster to the lath with screws and plaster washers. Fill any nail holes with spackle or patching plaster, let dry, and sand smooth. Damaged areas larger than 12 inches square may require professional repair.

Scrub dirt and grease from the wall with a solution of TSP or a wall cleaner designed for faux finishes. If the wall has been painted a light color, you'll probably only need to prime the repaired areas. But if you are changing from a dark painted finish to a light one, prime the entire wall. Plaster accessories like pots or sculpted pieces are extremely porous, so after cleaning with a tack cloth (not water), apply several base coats of gesso. Gesso, often used as the undercoating for artists' paintings on canvas, is available at art supply stores.

REPAIRING A CRACK

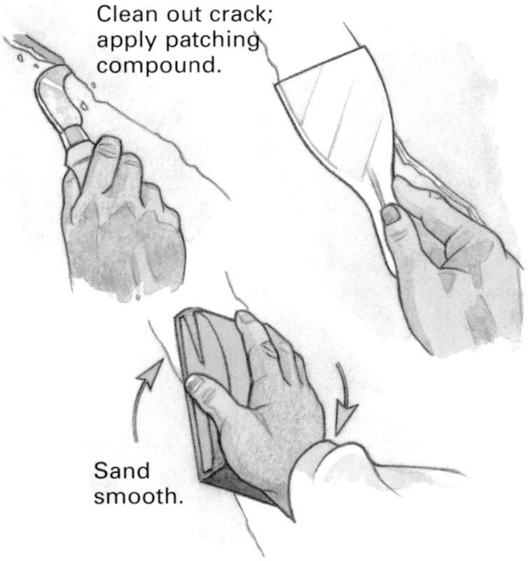

REPAIRING HOLES IN PLASTER

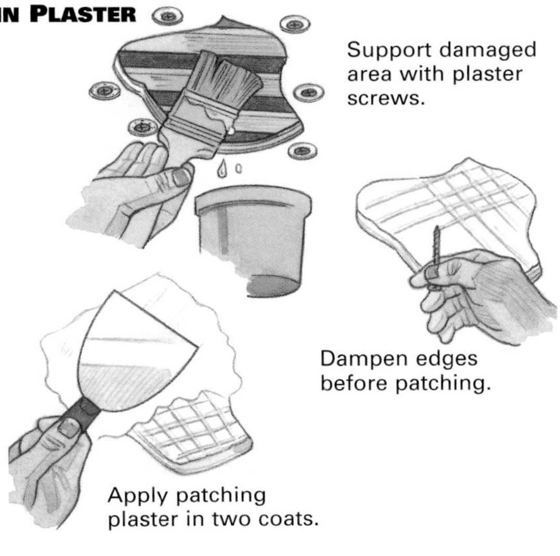

Support damaged area with plaster screws.
Dampen edges before patching.
Apply patching plaster in two coats.

PLASTER SCREWS

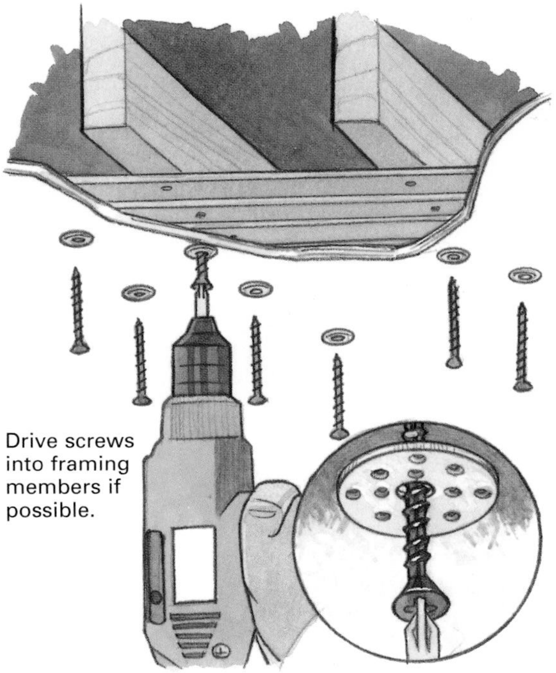

Drive screws into framing members if possible.

PREPARING FOR PAINTING

continued

PATCHING WITH REINFORCING TAPE

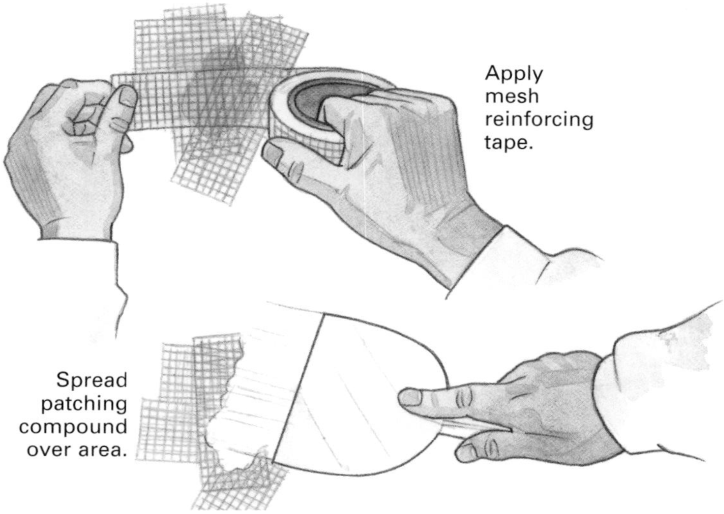

DRYWALL PATCH

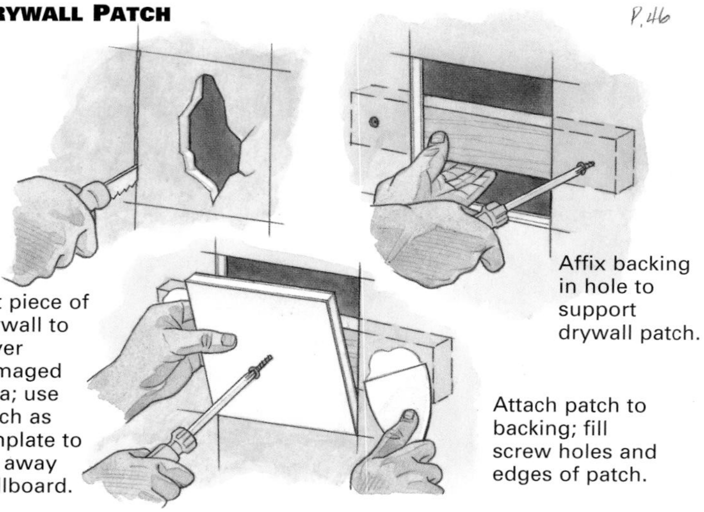

Affix backing in hole to support drywall patch.
Cut piece of drywall to cover damaged area; use patch as template to cut away wallboard.
Attach patch to backing; fill screw holes and edges of patch.

REPAIRING LARGE AREA

Cut piece of drywall to span from center to center on wall studs outside damaged area; use patch as template to cut away wallboard.
Attach patch to studs; fill screw holes and edges of patch.

DRYWALL: Little preparation is needed for new drywall other than light sanding and making sure all the dust is vacuumed away. Depending on the finish you apply, use either a primer or a primer-sealer before putting on the base coat.

You can usually paint right over old drywall that's been previously painted if the old paint is sound. Fill nail holes and repair any damage, as shown at left. Wash the wall to ensure that the new paint will stick to it.

MASONRY WALLS: Scrub masonry walls with a wire brush and TSP. Remove any alkali deposits with a mixture of muriatic acid and water. Wearing full-length rubber gloves and goggles, pour 1 part muriatic acid into 3 parts of water. (Always add acid to water; doing the opposite can cause dangerous bubbling and splashing.) Scrub the surface with a brush dipped into the acid solution. Rinse with water and let dry.

Apply a penetrating sealer to the surface as soon as possible after the acid solution dries. Masonry surface conditioner, sold by paint dealers, seals and hardens both unpainted masonry and masonry covered with aging paint. If the surface has flaking paint, scrub it off with TSP and a scrub brush.

WALLPAPER: Professionals usually recommend removing old wallpaper instead of painting over it. Painting over wallpaper is a quick fix, but removing it will yield a better paint job and will save you from having to remove painted wallpaper at some time in the future. Embossed designs or surface texture on the wallpaper will show through the paint. Wet removal using a solution containing enzymes is messy but also is the most effective method of stripping wallpaper.

If you do decide to paint over wallpaper, make sure the wallcovering is firmly bonded to the wall. Dry-sand the surface with a 150-grit open-mesh sanding cloth to smooth any irregularities and rough up the surface so the paint will adhere. Dust the surface, then apply two thin coats of sealer, such as KILZ or undercoater, to the wall. When dry, base-coat.

METAL: Metal surfaces, such as kitchen cabinets, usually are too smooth and slick for paint. Light sanding with 100- or 150-grit sandpaper will provide tooth for paint. Apply a metal primer before any paint.

There are a variety of rust removers and paint removers available for stripping a metal surface. Follow the manufacturer's directions and make sure all traces of these are washed off and that the surface is thoroughly dry before you begin priming or base-coating.

PLASTIC: Paint doesn't adhere very well to some plastics; that's one of the reasons plastic painting tools are so popular. Sand rigid plastics to break the surface glaze, then spray on a general-purpose primer from an aerosol can. Before spraying the whole item, test the primer on a hidden spot to make sure it will adhere to the plastic and won't craze the surface. Apply thin coats. Acrylic crafts paints adhere to some plastics. Paints made for plastic models, available at hobby shops in spray or brush-on form, come in many colors and work well.

STUCCO: Usually found on exterior walls, stucco is very porous. Coat it with a primer-sealer prior to painting. Any swirling or raised textures intentionally created when the stucco was applied will be difficult, if not impossible to hide, so make sure the final finish you want makes use of these textures.

TERRA-COTTA: Lightly sand clay and terra-cotta surfaces, then apply a sealer. Prime the surface to hide the dark earth color if you plan to paint the item a light color.

REPAIRING A CRACK

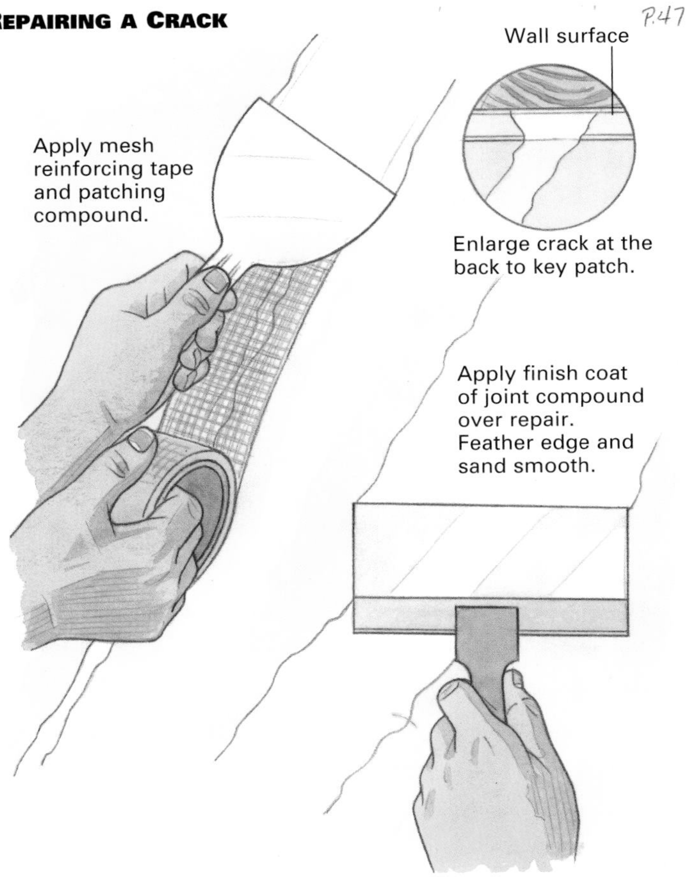

Wall surface
Apply mesh reinforcing tape and patching compound.
Enlarge crack at the back to key patch.
Apply finish coat of joint compound over repair. Feather edge and sand smooth.

CLEANING STUBBORN STAINS

Don't try to paint over stains; they will probably show through your new paint. If stains remain after you wash the wall, try these techniques to get rid of them.

MOLD AND MILDEW: Spots that look like splotches of dirt on your walls might be mold or mildew. These fungi thrive on surfaces in warm, damp rooms with poor ventilation. To test for mold or mildew, dab household bleach onto the spot. If the spot comes off, it's mold or mildew.

To remove mold or mildew, mix two teaspoons of dishwashing detergent with ⅔ cup of baking soda, 1 cup of household bleach, and a gallon of warm water. Wear gloves and goggles as you apply the solution with a damp mop; let stand for several minutes. Rinse with a solution of 1 cup vinegar and a gallon of water. When dry, lightly sand the places where the mildew appeared and seal against reinfection by applying two coats of white-pigmented sealer, sanding between coats.

GREASY STAINS: Rub a stubborn grease stain with a liquid deglosser to break the oil film. When dry, sand the cleaned area with 120-grit sandpaper, then wipe away the sanding dust. Seal the surface with two coats of white-pigmented sealer, sanding between coats.

RUST AND WATER STAINS: Rust and water stains will show through new paint. To remove them, repair any disintegrated areas, then scrub with a solution of 2 tablespoons of TSP mixed with a cup of warm water. Rinse with a mixture of 1 cup vinegar in a gallon of warm water. Allow to dry for several days, then sand with 120-grit paper. Seal with two coats of white-pigmented sealer, sanding between coats.

MARKER AND CRAYON STAINS: Heat a crayon mark with a hair dryer and blot away as much of the mark as possible. For permanent markers, lightly dab the spot with nail polish remover. Rub the spot with a liquid deglosser. When dry, sand with 120-grit paper, then wipe away the sanding dust. Seal with two coats of white-pigmented sealer, sanding between coats.

ADHESIVE: To remove paneling adhesive, scrape or chisel off as much of it as possible. Lightly sand, then apply two coats of sealer. Spackle the surface, then seal again. To remove wallpaper adhesive, use a wallpaper remover that has enzymes. Follow the remover manufacturer's instructions for mixing and use.

POINTERS ON PAINTING

PAINTING WITH A BRUSH

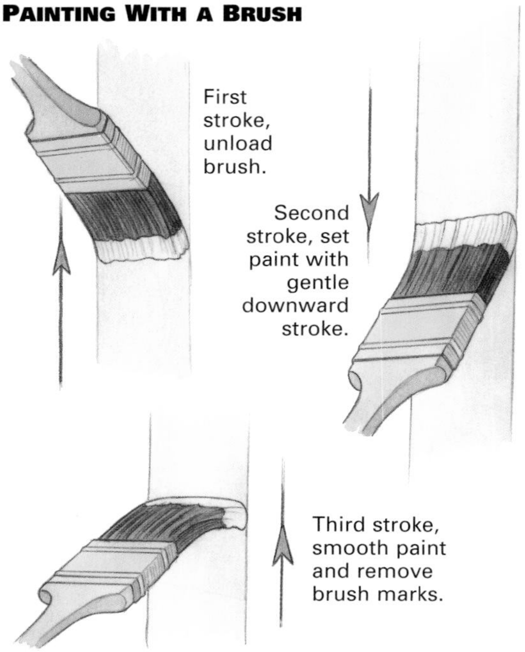
First stroke, unload brush.
Second stroke, set paint with gentle downward stroke.
Third stroke, smooth paint and remove brush marks.

Base-coating a wall is essentially the same as putting a coat of paint on it. For best results when painting all the walls in a room, follow a specific sequence. First empty the room, or at least move all the furniture away from the walls and to the middle of the room. Cover the furniture and the floor, and mask the trim.

If you plan to paint the ceiling and the walls, start with the ceiling, then proceed to the walls and trim. Base-coating is an ideal job for two people: one can do the cutting in with a brush or pad while the other paints the surfaces with a roller.

PAINTING WITH A ROLLER

Second stroke, set the paint.
First stroke, unload roller.
Third stroke, smooth the paint.

CUTTING IN

Painters cut in—paint the edge of a surface up to an adjoining surface—with a brush or pad because a roller can't do the job neatly. Trying to paint into a corner with a roller usually results in a messy job. To cut in, paint a 3- to 4-inch-wide band along both sides of the inside corner between a ceiling and wall or along a surface adjacent to trim or molding.

One of the biggest mistakes in painting is cutting in an entire room, then rolling the walls. Doing this allows most of the cut-in bands to dry before you paint the wall, creating visible overlaps in the finish. To avoid a visible overlap, keep a wet edge where you cut in so the paint flows together between the cutting-in line and the rest of the wall. The wall will then dry at the same rate for a uniform look.

A paint pad is probably the easiest tool to use for cutting in a wall or ceiling. The pad will lay more paint on the surface than a brush. It also minimizes brush strokes and covers a surface much faster than brushing.

To load a paint pad, dip it in its tray, wiggle it around, and pat the pad to remove excess. To cut in, place the pad against the edge of the surface, and glide it along the corner.

BRUSHING PAINT

Start at the left bottom corner of a wall and paint from the bottom up with strokes about 16 to 18 inches long. Here's how to apply the paint in three strokes for a smooth job:

- Unload the brush or pad with the first upward stroke.
- Set the paint with a gentle stroke downward over the first.
- Smooth the paint with a gentle upward stroke to remove brush marks. Feather the end and edge of the stroke and keep them wet to prevent distinct lines from developing between strokes.

Continue moving up and around the wall using this technique. When you have painted from the bottom of the wall to the top, make a final continuous upward stroke to eliminate transition lines and brush marks.

ROLLING ON PAINT

As with a brush, it is important to keep a wet edge when painting with a roller. Hold the roller so the U-shaped end is away from the direction you are working. Work in small sections, loading the roller with paint, then rolling up and down until the entire surface is covered. Work vertically from floor to ceiling. Roll on paint with three strokes in this way:

- Unload the roller with an upward stroke.
- Set the paint with a gentle stroke down.
- Finish with a light upward stroke to smooth the paint and remove lines called snail trails.

Twisting the roller handle slightly in the direction you are working—normally to the right—will also help eliminate lines. To keep the sheen consistent, lay off the paint by lightly rolling a damp roller from top to bottom across the wall.

PAINTING DOORS

Doors are often painted with dramatic faux-finish wood grains. The easiest way to paint a door is to paint it in its frame. Remove the striker plate, doorknobs, and other hardware, but leave the lock mechanism and hinges in place. Clean the lock and hinges with rubbing alcohol, then apply two thin coats of rubber cement to mask them.

FLUSH DOORS: Base-coat from left to right with a roller, beginning on the inside of the room with the door closed. Smooth the paint by rolling upward. Paint around all sides of the door. When the paint is thoroughly dry, score around the edges of the hinges and the lock with a knife and gently rub the rubber cement from the hardware.

PANELED DOORS: Paint the base coat on paneled doors with a brush. Paint the panels first, starting with the panel moldings, moving to the recessed edge of the panel, and finishing with the face. Paint the center stiles (vertical members) and center rails (horizontal members) next. Paint the top and bottom rails, then the left and right stiles.

CABINETRY

If you are painting a cabinet, paint the interior first. The interior usually gets a coat of enamel in a color that complements the decorative finish, but doesn't receive the decorative finish itself.

To paint the interior of a cabinet with adjustable shelves, remove the shelves and lay them flat for easier painting. Let each surface dry completely before painting the next.

1. Begin with the underside and back edge, then paint the top and leading edge.
2. Paint the interior face of cabinet doors, then the leading edges.
3. Remove drawers and stand them on their backs. The drawer front will receive the decorative finish later; do not paint the drawer or the drawer openings inside the cabinet.
4. Paint the inside back wall, sidewalls, and floor of the cabinet.
5. Then paint the exterior with the decorative finish. Start with the front and sides, then paint the doors and top. Paint the drawer fronts and leading edges.

On a cabinet with nonremovable shelves, start at the back of the cabinet and move forward. If the cabinet has drawers, remove them. Paint the back wall first, followed by the shelf bottoms. Paint the sidewalls and shelf tops next, along with the leading edges of the shelves. Paint the floor of the cabinet next. Then paint the cabinet ends, face frame rails and stiles, the inside and edges of the door, and the toe-kick. With the drawers standing on their backs, paint the fronts.

PAINTING A PANEL

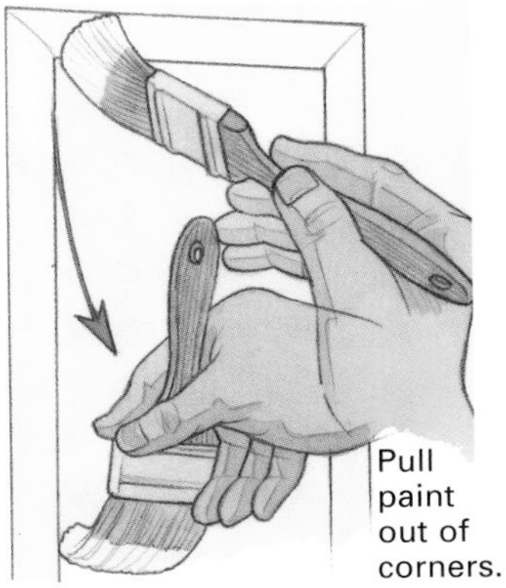

PAINTING A PANELED DOOR

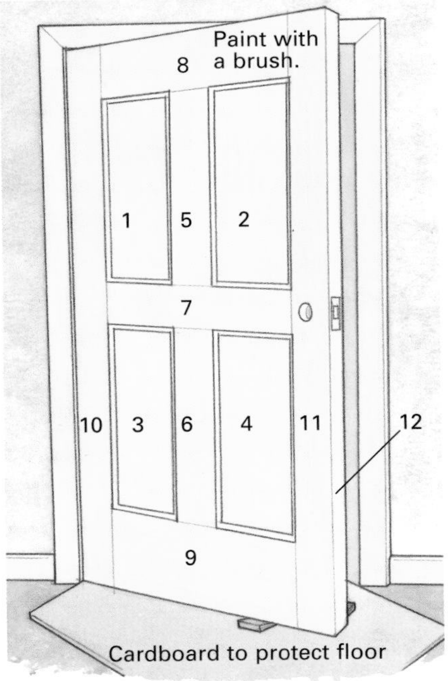

Numbers show painting sequence.

PAINTING A CABINET

Numbers show painting sequence.

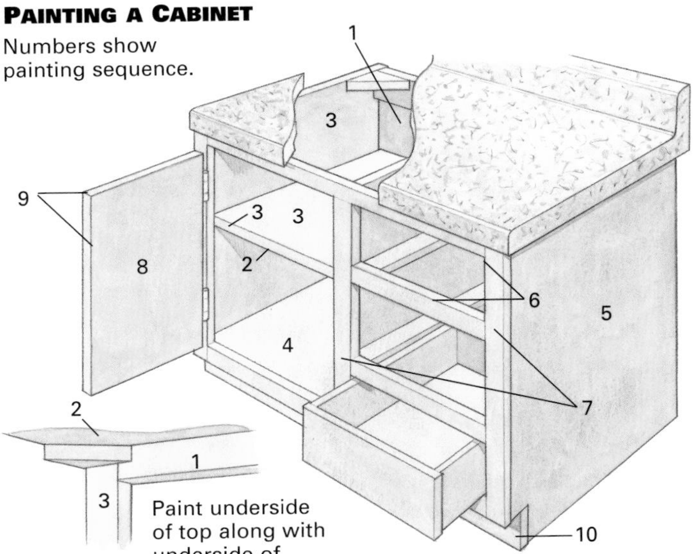

Remove drawers; paint fronts only.

PAINTING TECHNIQUES

IN THIS SECTION

HOW THIS SECTION WORKS

This chapter begins with the Gallery of Effects—photos of some popular decorative paint techniques and faux finishes painted by artist Susan Goans Driggers. A page reference with each photo directs you to instructions for painting the finish. A chart like the one at right indicates the relative complexity of each finish—more brushes indicate techniques with more steps. Complex techniques may take more time or care to apply, but they usually are not more difficult to accomplish than others. Boxes like the ones at right appear with the instructions to provide information about the tools and materials needed and to offer suggestions about where to use the finish.

With care and patience, you can paint any of the finishes shown. Practice is the key to success. Before you start painting the living room walls or the fireplace surround in the family room, practice painting the finish on a piece of plywood, drywall, poster board, or similar material. A piece between 18 inches and 2 feet square makes a good practice board. Base-coat the board, then follow the instructions for the technique. If you make mistakes, paint over the board and try again. (You can do this when you paint the project too.) As you become more comfortable with the tools and materials, you will gain the confidence that brings success.

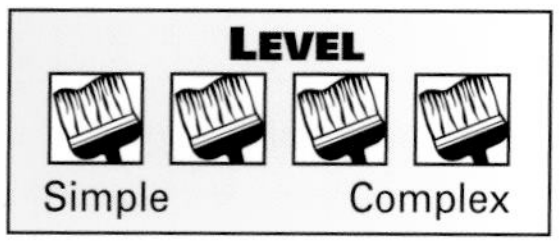

SUPPLIES

This box accompanying each technique tells you what materials and tools you will need. (The tools and materials are illustrated in the chapter that begins on page 18.) Some techniques will work on walls, furniture, or small objects, so some tool choices will depend on the scale of your project. A standard paint roller would be fine for base-coating a wall, for instance, but it would be better to use a small craft-painting roller or a brush to base-coat a small desk box.

WORKS WONDERS ON...

This box with each technique suggests where to apply a particular finish. Some finishes are better used on a large surface, such as a wall. Others work best as highlights or accents—on a door, a mantel, or for trim, for instance. Some seem most appropriate on small objects, such as a desk box. The suggestions are simply guides; consider them as you look at the photo of the finished technique to decide if that finish is the one you want.

GALLERY OF EFFECTS

GLAZING AND COLOR WASHING

Instructions on page 50

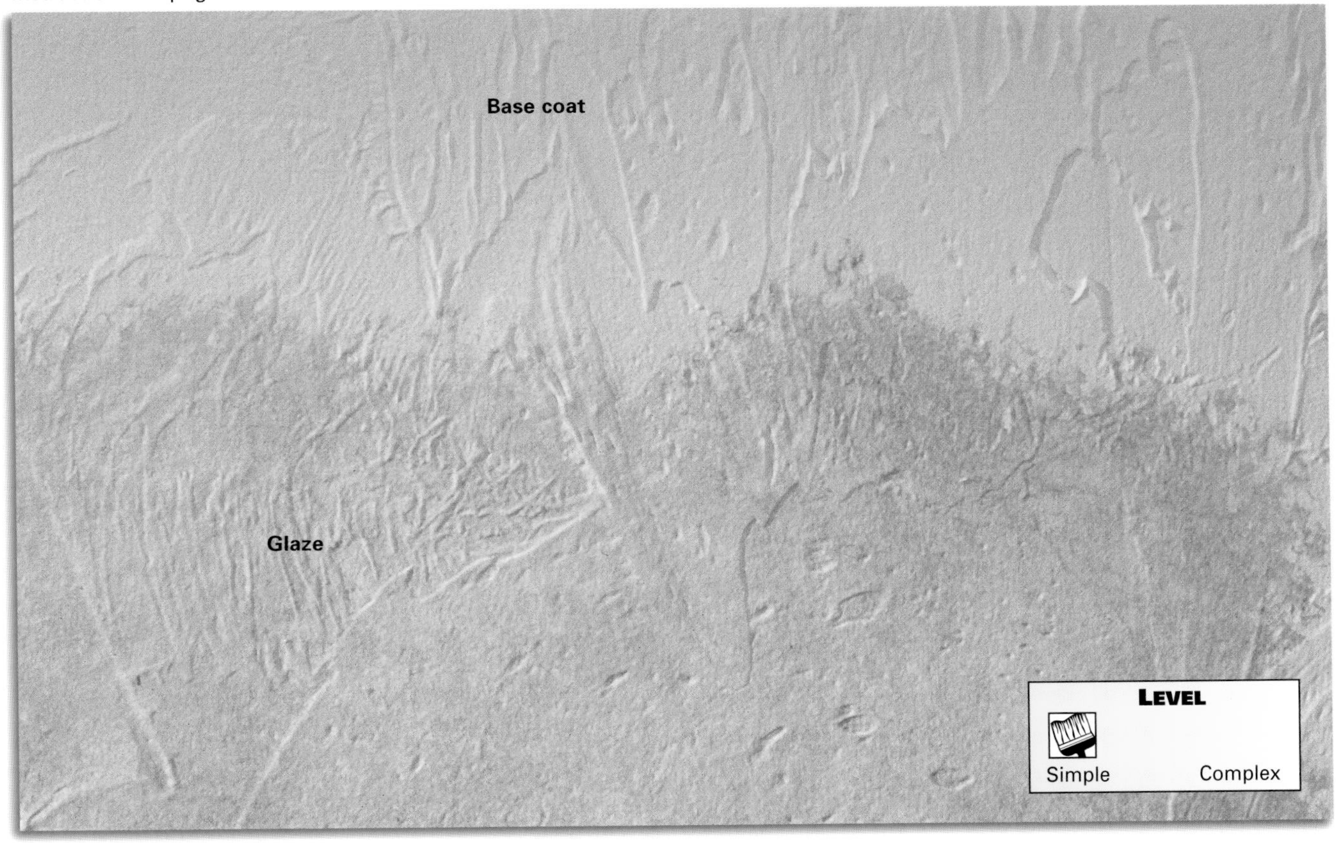

ANTIQUING AND AGING

Instructions on page 52

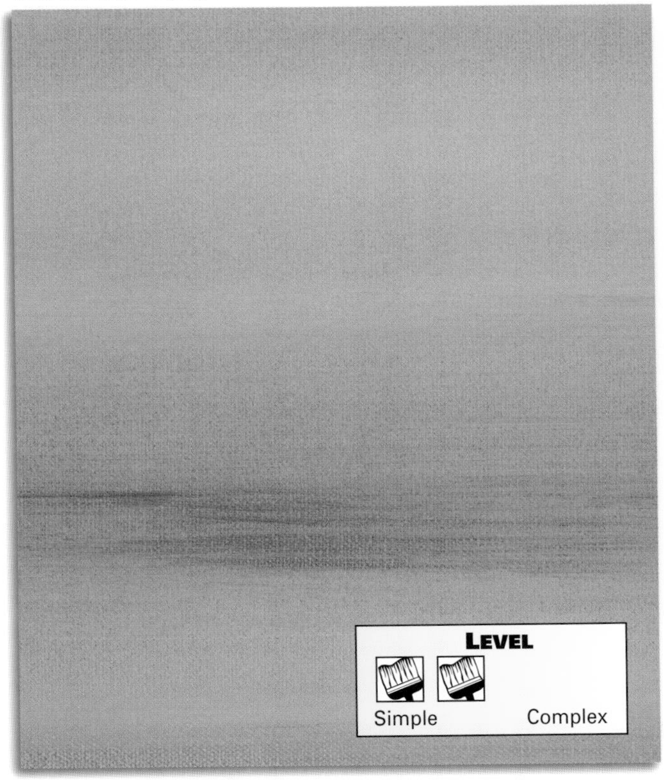

COMBING

Instructions on page 54

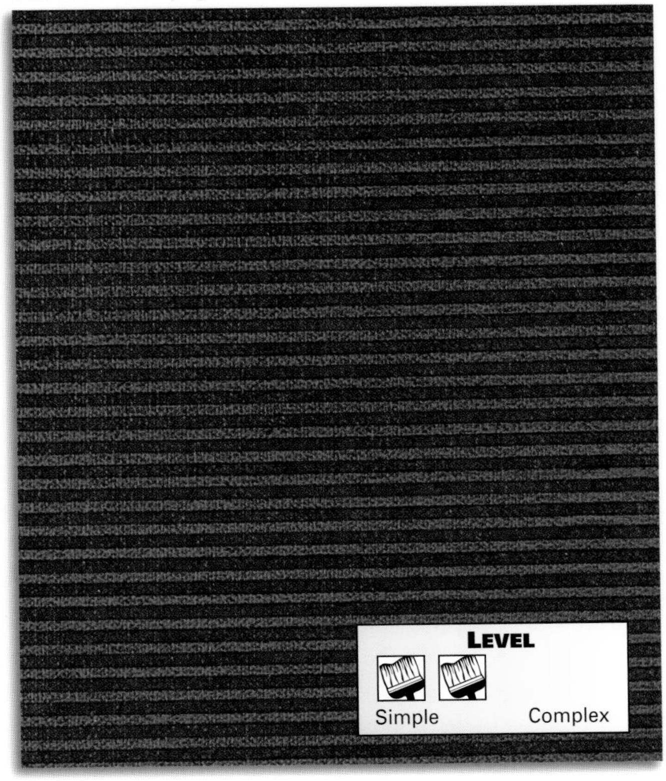

GALLERY OF EFFECTS

continued

CRACKLING

Instructions on page 56

DISTRESSING

Instructions on page 58

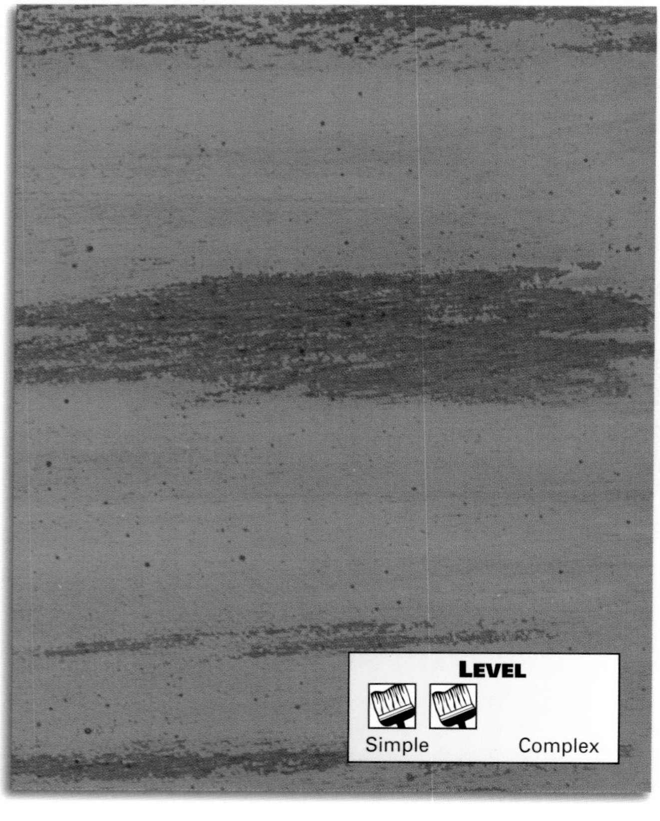

DRAGGING

Instructions on page 60

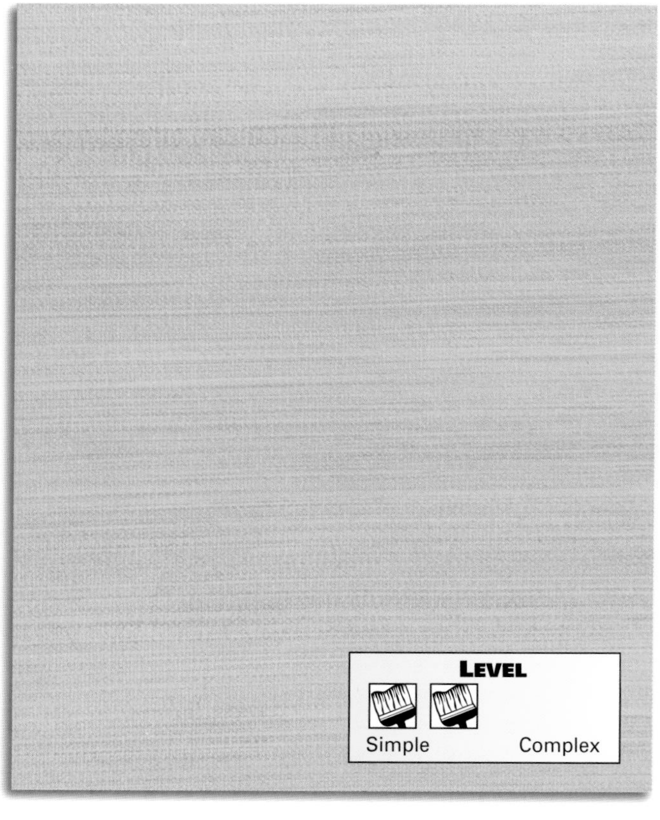

FLOGGING

Instructions on page 62

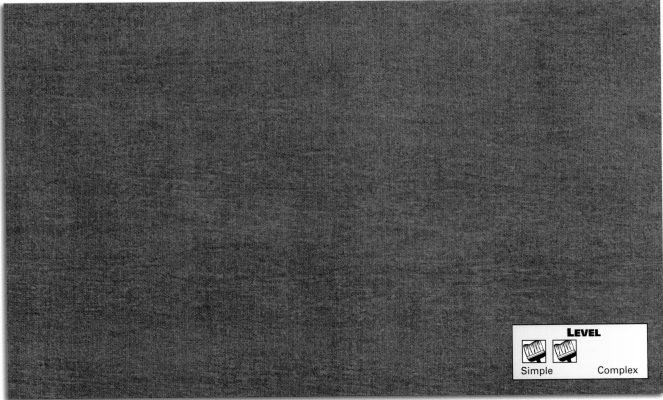

GOLD LEAFING

Instructions on page 64

WOOD GRAINING

Instructions on page 66

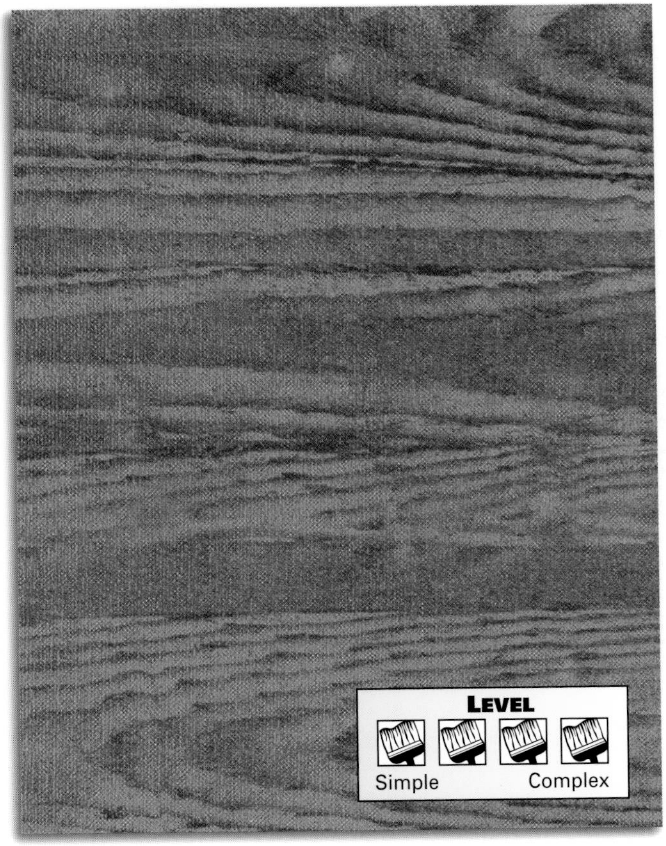

GALLERY OF EFFECTS
continued

GRANITE
Instructions on page 68

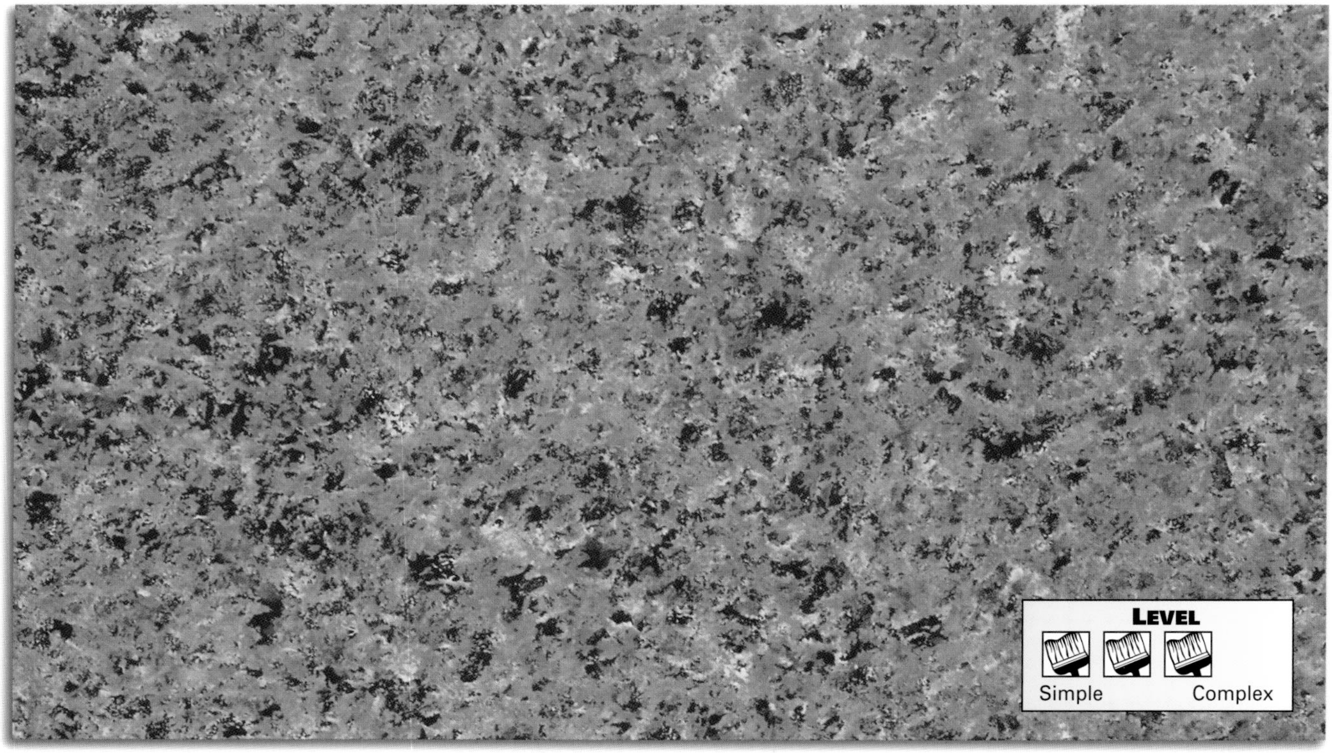

MALACHITE
Instructions on page 70

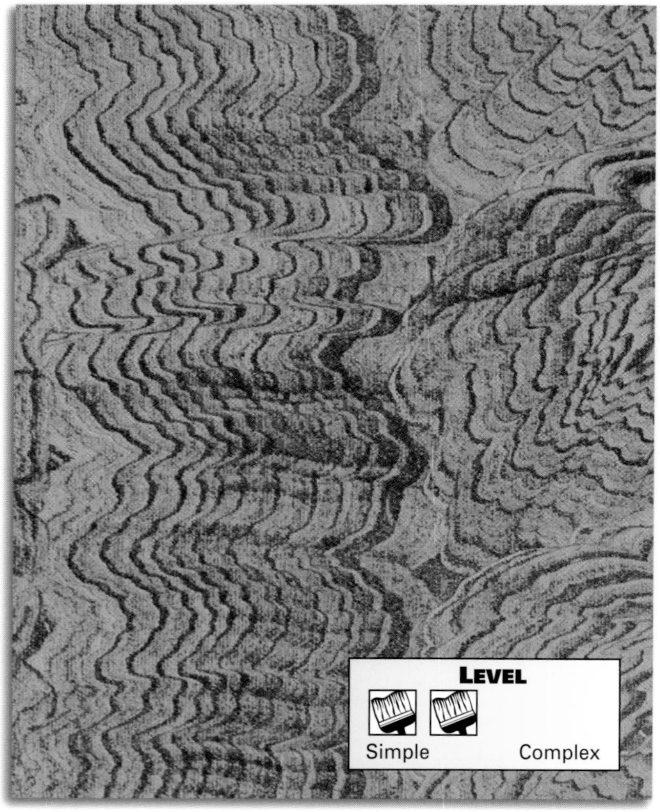

MARBLING
Instructions on page 72

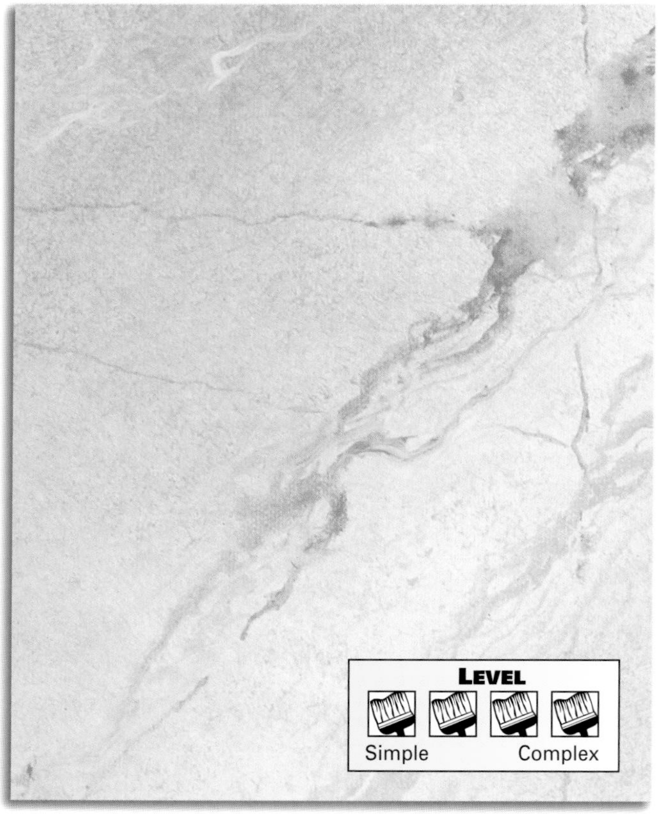

RAGGING

Instructions on page 74

SPATTERING

Instructions on page 76

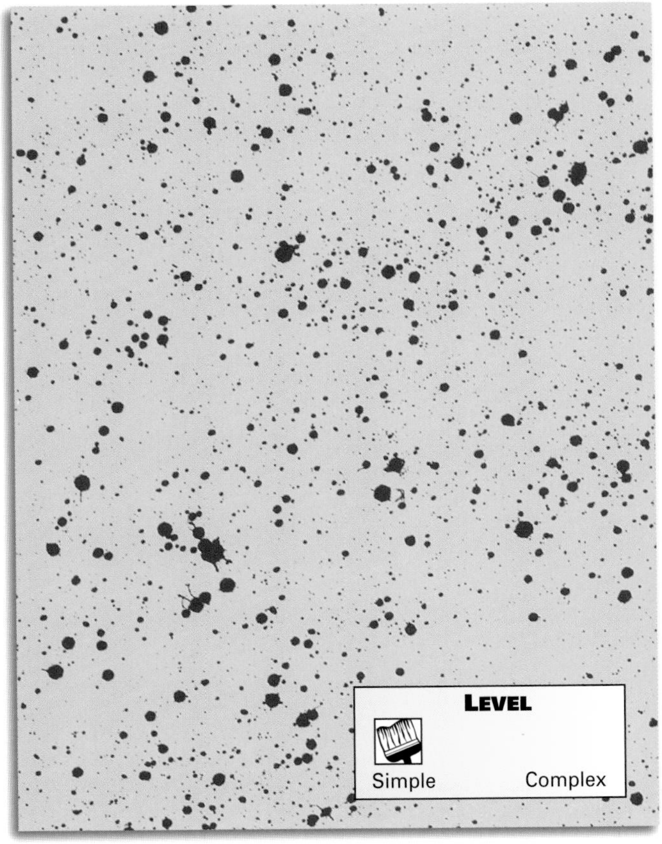

SPONGING

Instructions on page 78

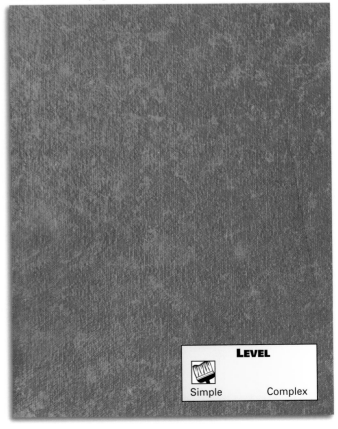

GALLERY OF EFFECTS
continued

STENCILING

Instructions on page 80

STIPPLING

Instructions on page 82

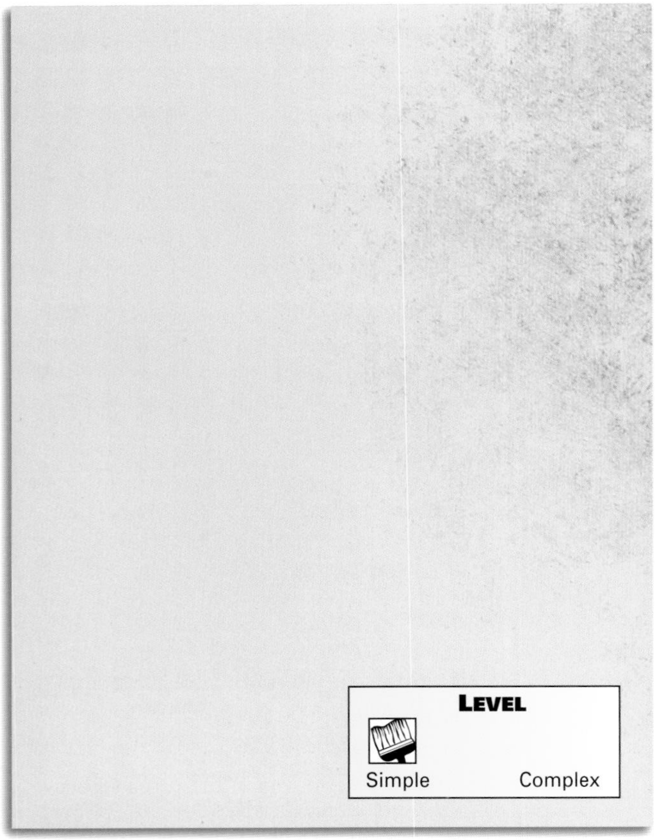

STONE BLOCKS AND BRICKS

Instructions on page 84

STRIPING
Instructions on page 86

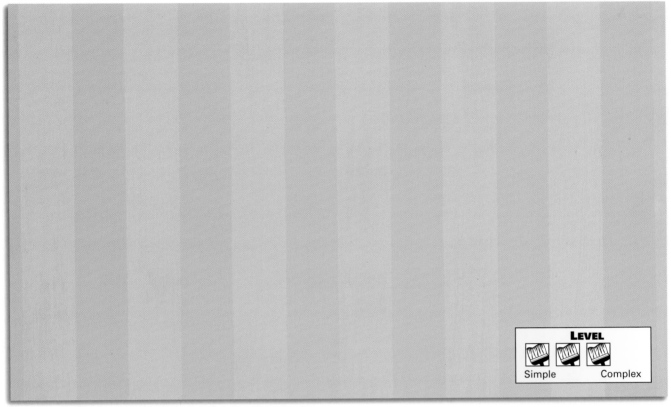

TORTOISESHELL
Instructions on page 88

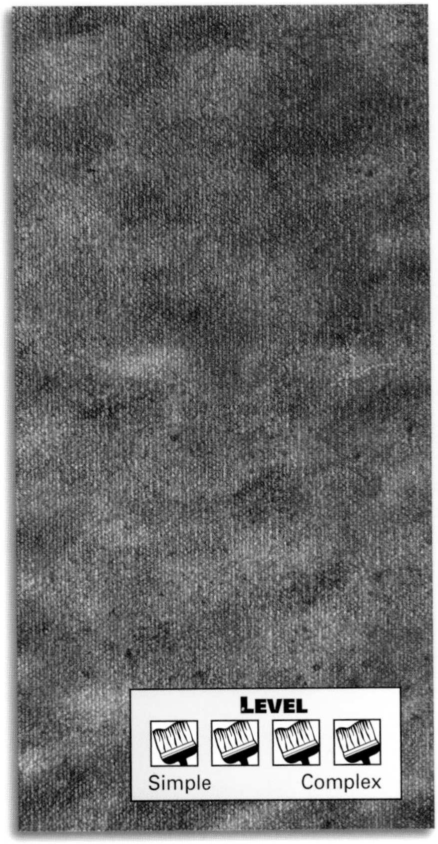

WEATHERED METAL: VERDIGRIS
Instructions on page 90

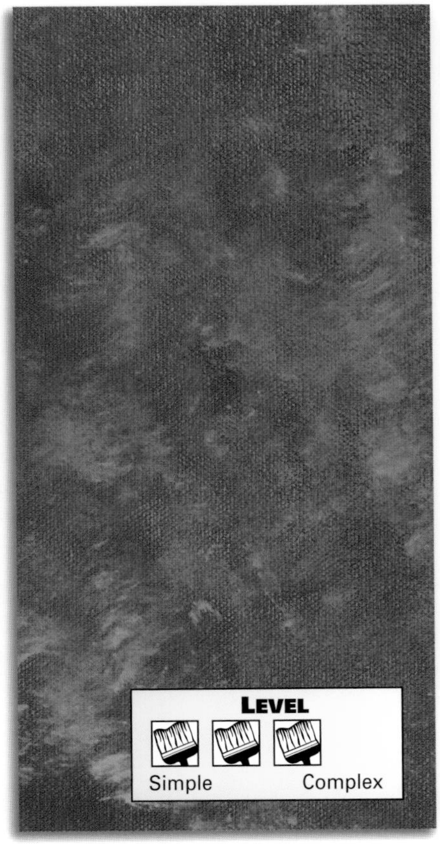

WEATHERED METAL: OXIDIZED IRON
Instructions on page 92

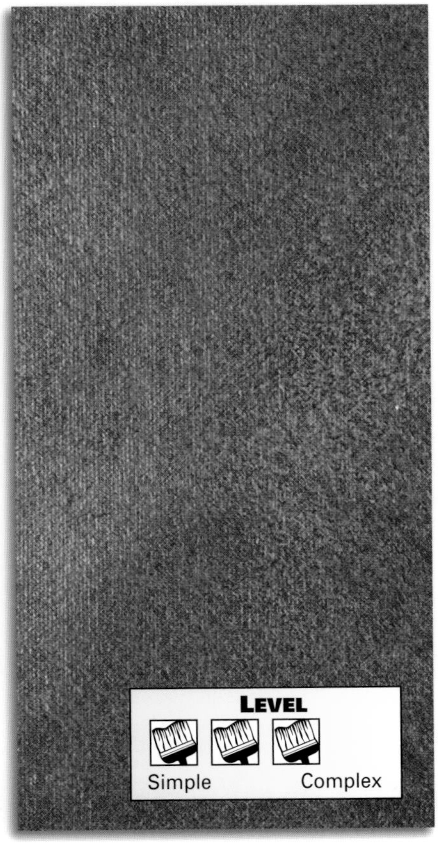

GLAZING AND COLOR WASHING

LEVEL

Simple — Complex

SUPPLIES

- Water-base or oil glazes
- Brushes, rags, cheesecloth, sponges, crumpled paper, or plastic wrap

WORKS WONDERS ON...

Glazes can create many decorative effects depending on the application. Glaze treatments are suitable for walls, furniture, woodwork, and small items.

Glazes are the basis of many decorative finishes. A glaze is a translucent color coat that gives decorative finishes their depth. Oil-base glazes have greater depth and color intensity as well as a longer open time (the time it remains wet on the wall). Water-base glazes dry more quickly, but clean up with soap and water.

Glazes can be applied two ways: negative application and positive application. In a negative application, glaze applied over the base coat is then removed in areas to expose the base coat, as shown at the top of the opposite page. Negative application generally results in stronger coloration and patterns.

In a positive application, glaze is brushed, sponged, or otherwise applied in a pattern over the base-coated surface, as shown in the photos at left. This usually results in tighter coloration and more subtle patterns. And you aren't limited to using a brush or sponge—everything from bubble wrap to crumpled paper will give you some kind of unique effect. Experiment with materials you have around the house.

A color wash is a positive glaze application with a brush or sponge that covers the entire surface, shown on the walls in the photo at the bottom of the opposite page. Color-washing over a neutral base coat is a good way to add color where a coat of paint would be too intense.

Apply glaze in thin, subtle layers of color rather than thick, distinct blotches. Here are some ways to treat glazes:

- Roll or dab cheesecloth on the surface for a fine texture in either positive or negative applications. Wash the cheesecloth first to soften it and remove lint.
- Create soft-edge effects with a sponge. Dampen the sponge with water to soften it before applying or removing glaze with it. (See page 78 for more about sponging.)
- Make a crinkled look with sharp lines by dabbing or rolling the glaze with crumpled paper. Use clean paper such as unprinted brown bags, butcher paper, or blank newsprint.
- Remove or apply glaze with bunched-up plastic wrap. To make markings that resemble plaster, apply larger sheets of plastic wrap to wet glazed walls; it will adhere and wrinkle on contact. Then, peel it away to reveal the markings.

Rolling glaze onto a wall with a rag (left) or dabbing it on with a sponge (below) are positive application techniques. Vinyl or latex gloves—not being worn here—will keep the messy glaze off your hands.

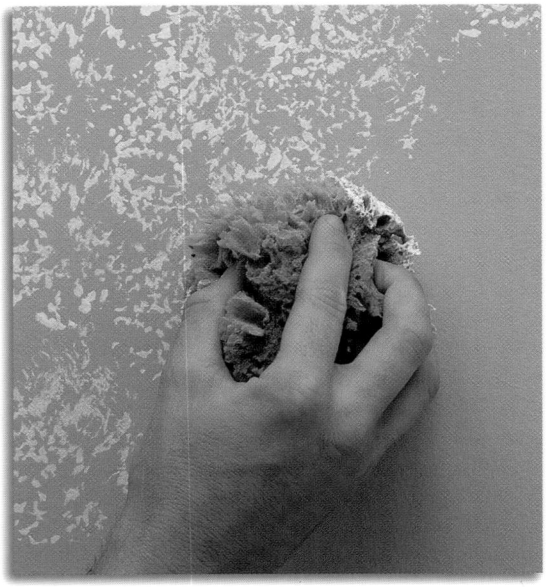

You can roll the base coat onto a wall like paint. Glaze is then brushed or rolled over the dried base coat for a negative application.

Glaze applied over the basecoat is then partially removed to create the decorative effect.

TEST THE TECHNIQUE FIRST

Before you start painting your project—especially when using a negative glaze technique—paint a poster board with the same base coat and glaze you will use. This will help you determine the glaze drying time so you'll know how large an area you can cover and how quickly you need to work before the glaze dries. Besides getting some practice in working with the finish technique, you'll get a look at your color combination before starting the project.

Slightly transparent glazes add color and depth to surfaces when applied as a color wash.

ANTIQUING AND AGING

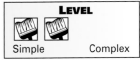

LEVEL

Simple — Complex

Burnt umber works well over most colors for antiquing and aging. It has been thinned here so it won't overpower the beige base coat.

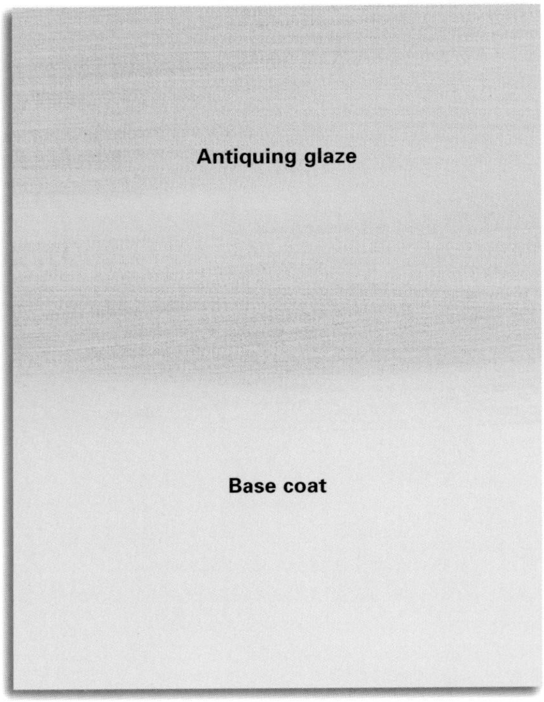

SUPPLIES

- Oil or acrylic colors and neutral glaze
- Mineral spirits (for oil paint only)
- Brush-on antiquing mixtures or stain
- Stirring stick
- Small paintbrush or sponge
- Rags

WORKS WONDERS ON...

Painted furniture is a natural for antiquing and aging. The technique works well on items such as picture or mirror frames and small accessories. Antiquing can be applied over walls and woodwork to age a room. Antiqued finishes fit well into country decorating schemes.

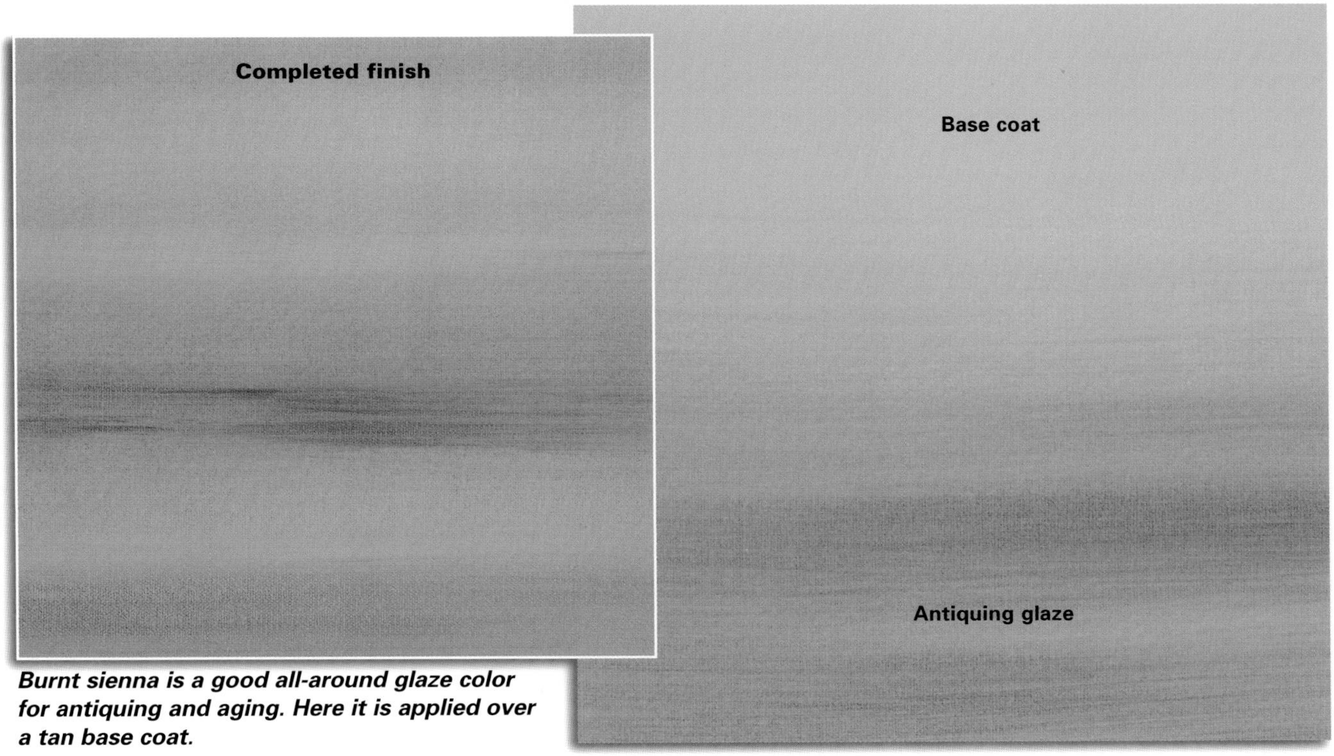

Burnt sienna is a good all-around glaze color for antiquing and aging. Here it is applied over a tan base coat.

An antique finish makes a piece of furniture or a room's walls or woodwork look older than they are. There are a number of commercial antiquing products available that produce different results. When you use one of them, follow the manufacturer's directions on the containers.

You can make your own antiquing mixture, using glazing medium and colored paint glaze, latex paint, acrylic paint, or oil paint. Glazing mediums are available for use with both oil-base and water-base paints. Make sure you use the right kind of glaze for the paint you choose. Oil-base products take longer to dry and give you more open—or working—time. Fast-drying acrylics are fine for small surfaces. Glaze extends the drying time of acrylics.

Mix colors in a pan or plastic tray and thin them to a soupy consistency using the right kind of thinner for the glaze and paint. The product label will guide you. Varying the thickness of the medium will help determine the degree of antiquing you achieve. A darker mixture less thinned by glaze will result in a more heavily antiqued look.

PROCEDURE: Seal the surface with varnish to help control the antiquing color. This is especially important for lightly antiqued surfaces. After the varnish dries, brush or sponge the antiquing over the surface. Wipe off unwanted antiquing color with a clean rag.

For walls, or for a heavily antiqued surface, you can apply the antiquing color directly onto the paint. Let the concentration of color in the glaze determine how heavy the antiquing color will be. One glaze application followed by one wiping-off will result in a light antiquing color. For more pronounced color, apply additional layers.

Allow the glaze to build up in the corners, joints, cracks, and details. Vary how much you wipe off and the areas you wipe for a more realistic simulation of aging.

Dark blue antiquing over a light blue base has been enhanced with spattering (***see page 76*** ***).***

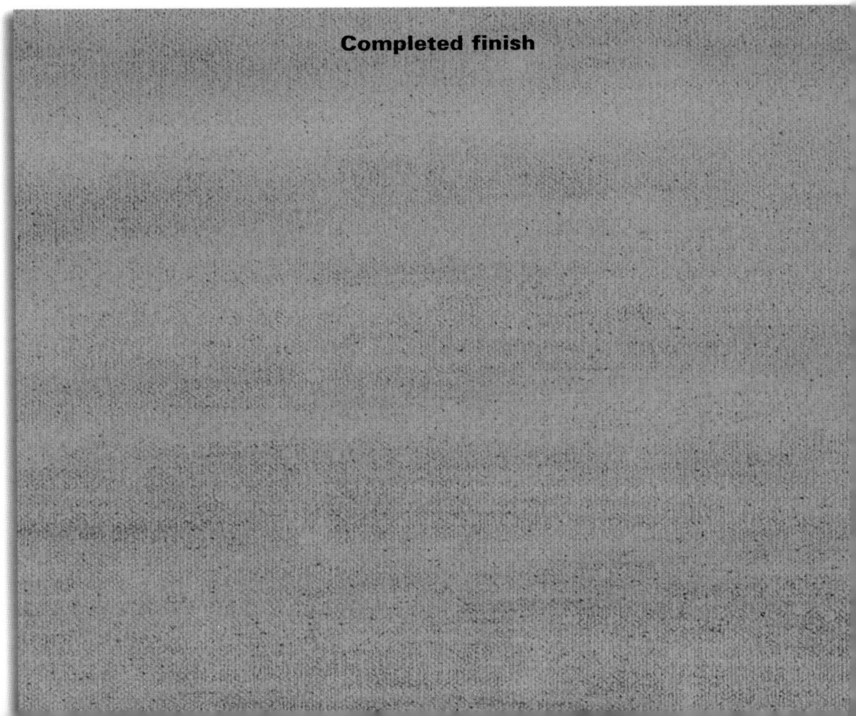

COMBING

LEVEL

Simple Complex

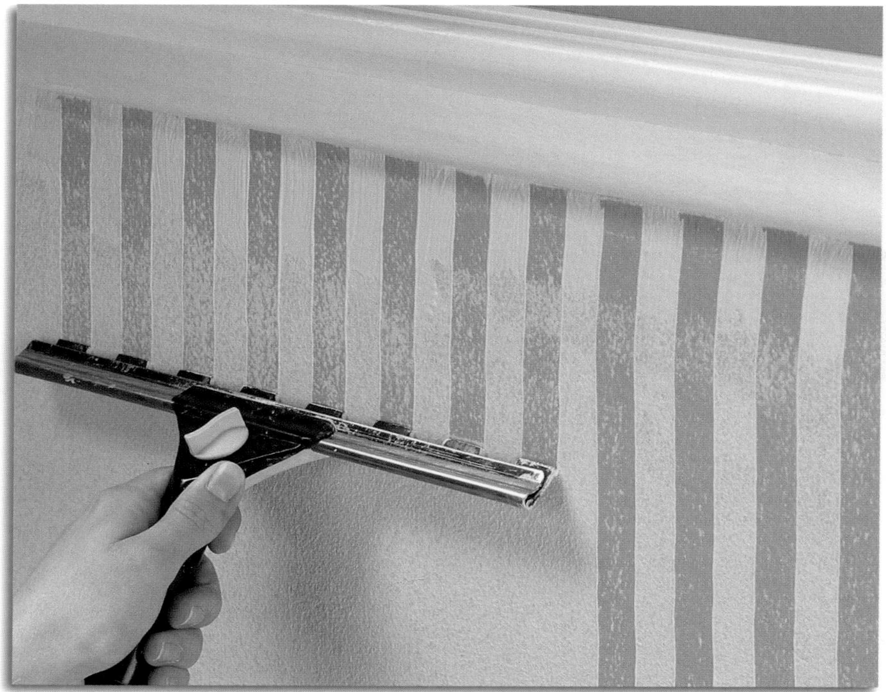

Squeegees are available for combing large surfaces. You can cut a custom pattern into a standard window-washing squeegee. Paint and crafts dealers sell combing tools like the ones below.

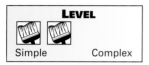

WORKS WONDERS ON...

Combing adapts easily to any size surface because you can vary the spacing between the teeth of the comb. A small, fine-toothed comb can make delicate patterns on small items. A window squeegee that has had notches cut into it is often used for larger areas such as a wall.

SUPPLIES

- Combing tools
- Neutral glazing medium
- Colored paint glaze
- Acrylic paint or latex wall paint

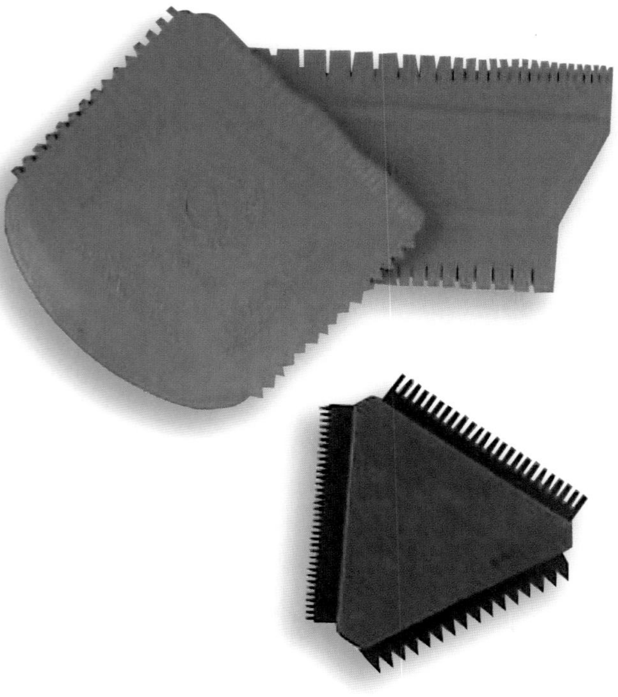

Combing is done by raking through a wet coat of colored glaze with various tools, allowing the base coat to show through in a pattern. The glaze dries slower than wet paint and allows you more open time (time before the medium dries). See Glazing on page 50.

Because it's a freehand technique, the design you create is ultimately up to you; the possibilities are endless. Practice on a spare panel or board to achieve the effect you want. Once you begin on your project surface, complete each pass with the comb in one nonstop motion. You will probably work small sections at a time, such as stripes or panels. Lifting up the combing tool prematurely will create a break in the pattern left by the comb's teeth that will be almost impossible to match if you try to continue it later.

PROCEDURE: Start by applying a base-coat color of your choice. Let it dry.

Mix glazing medium with paint, following the medium manufacturer's directions. A 50-50 mix of paint and glaze is usually a good starting point.

Working in one area at a time, brush or roll on the glaze. While the glaze is wet, pull the comb through it to create the pattern. Wipe off the comb with a damp cloth often. If you work quickly, you can brush over any unwanted comb marks and re-comb the design.

While the glaze is wet, you can soften and blend the lines by stippling (see page 82) or flogging (see page 62).

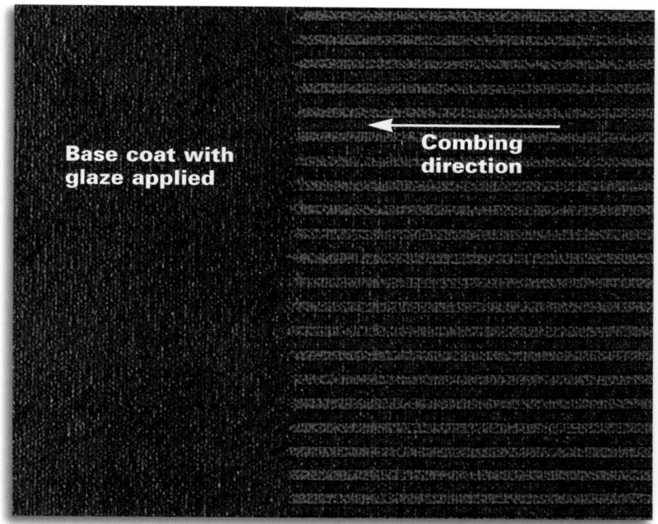

A tool with evenly spaced teeth makes uniform, parallel lines. You can comb horizontally, vertically, or at an angle in straight or wavy lines.

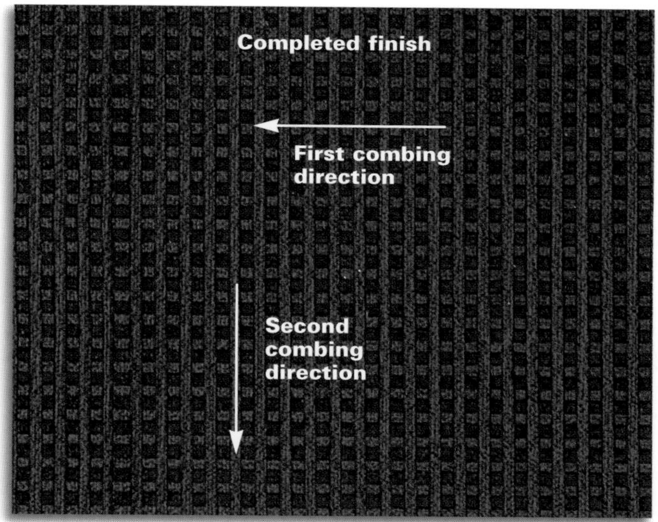

Comb twice at right angles to create a crosshatch pattern. The continuous lines will run in the direction of the second pass. You could comb at other angles too.

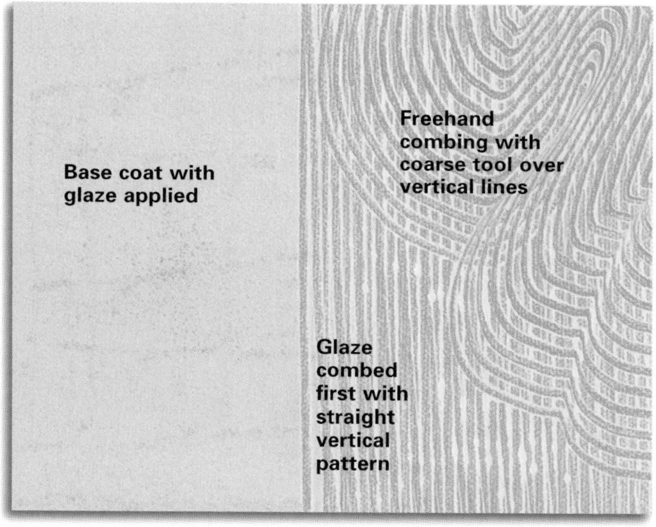

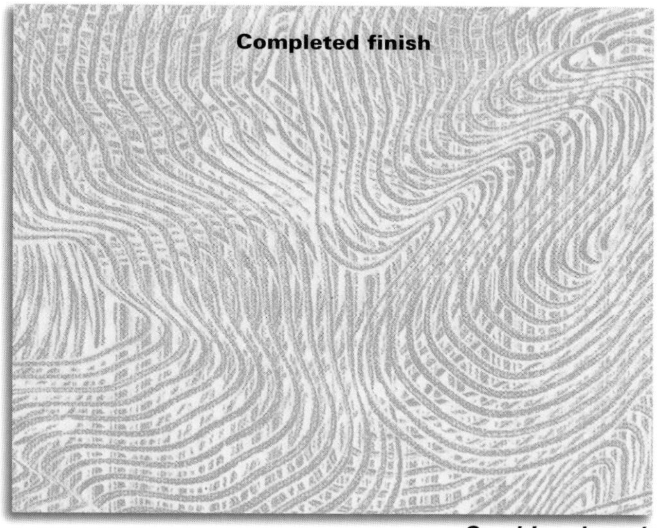

Combing doesn't have to look linear. Freehand combing over a straight background makes a striking finish.

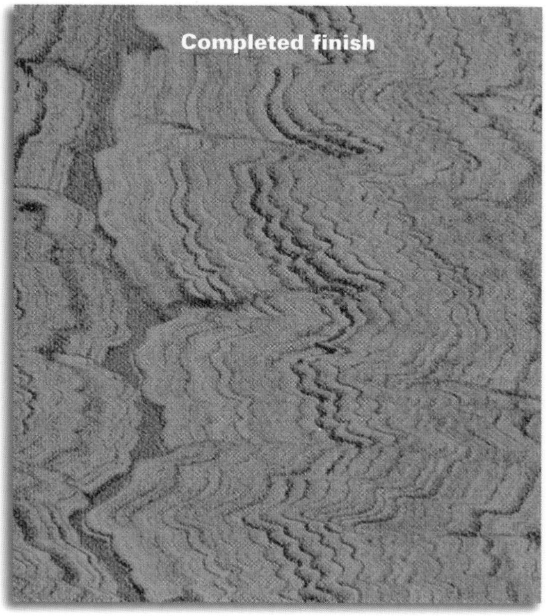

Freehand combing using a tool with graduated teeth results in a random-looking pattern. The green pattern resembles the mineral malachite *(see page 70).*

CRACKLING

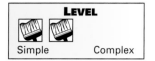

LEVEL

Simple Complex

Paint applied over crackle medium cracks as it dries.

Crackle mediums come in many easy-to-apply varieties and offer a wide range of final finishes. Some create cracks that are broad and obvious; others are finer and more subtle. Many mediums are applied over the base coat and cause the top coat of paint to crackle. Other products are two-part finishes which are applied over each other and crackle as they dry. You can enhance those finishes by rubbing antiquing glaze or paint into the cracks.

To create a two-color effect, apply the first color as the base coat. When thoroughly dry, brush on the crackle medium and let dry. Use a clean, dry brush to apply the second color, which will crackle as it dries, revealing the base-coat color in the cracks.

In general, the thinner the layer of crackle medium, the finer the cracks. The direction of the cracks that appear generally follows the direction you brush the top coat. This is especially important when working on a large area. You may want to apply your paint with random brushing, which will result in a less linear crackling pattern.

PROCEDURE: Base-coat the surface with one to three coats of paint. Let dry.

Brush crackle medium over the painted surface and let dry. It should

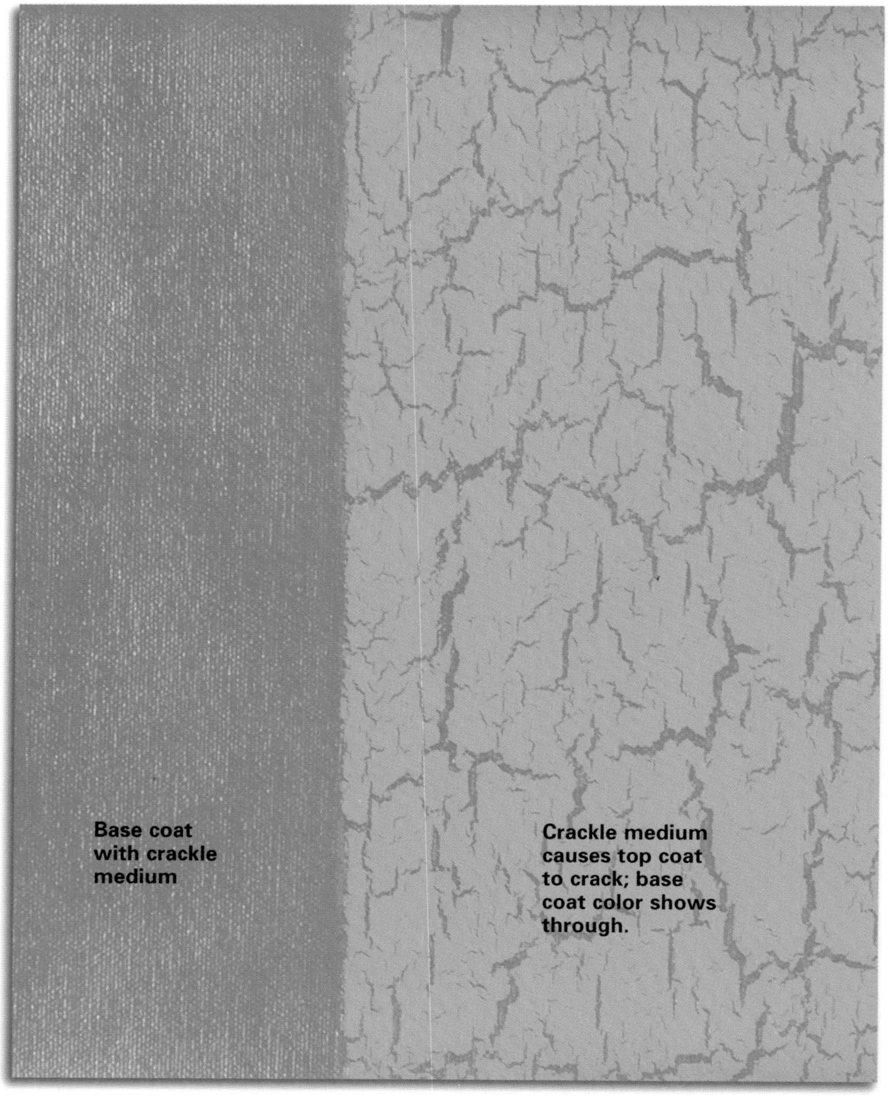
Base coat with crackle medium
Crackle medium causes top coat to crack; base coat color shows through.

SUPPLIES

- Latex wall paint
- Crackle medium
- Brush-on clear varnish
- Foam brush
- Cellulose sponge

WORKS WONDERS ON...

This technique works well on small items, furniture, or woodwork. Experiment with the materials on scrap wood to be sure the size and pattern of the crackling is appropriate for the surface.

Crackling makes the doors in this new home look like they've weathered many years.

look shiny; if it doesn't, apply a second coat. Let the crackle medium dry.

Using a clean, dry brush, apply a coat of water-base paint. (You can make a clear cracked surface over the base color by brushing water-base varnish over the crackle medium.) Cracks will begin to form as you brush on the top coat.

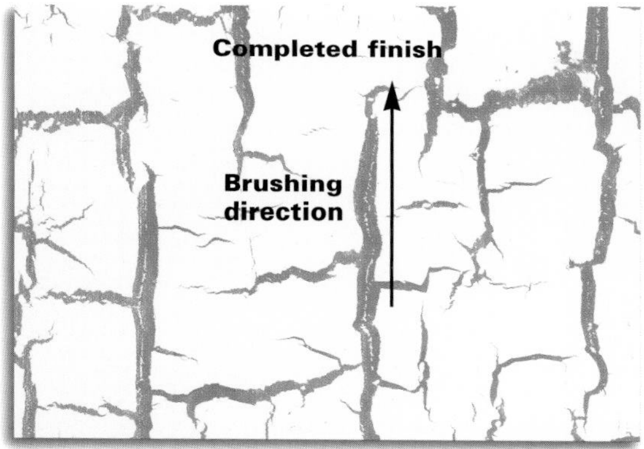

These large cracks result from brushing the top paint coat in one direction.

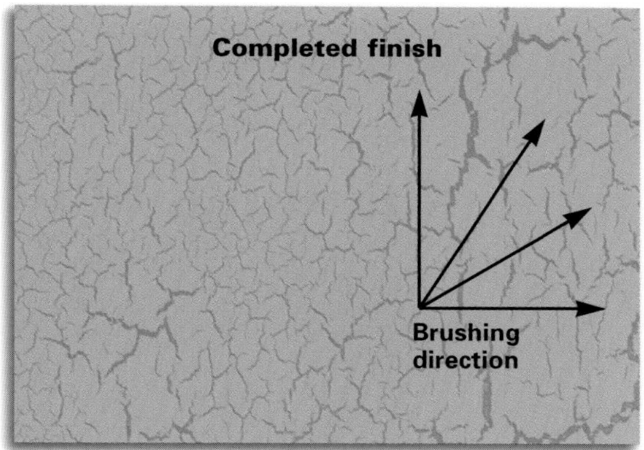

Brushing in several directions makes fine to medium cracks in the top color coat.

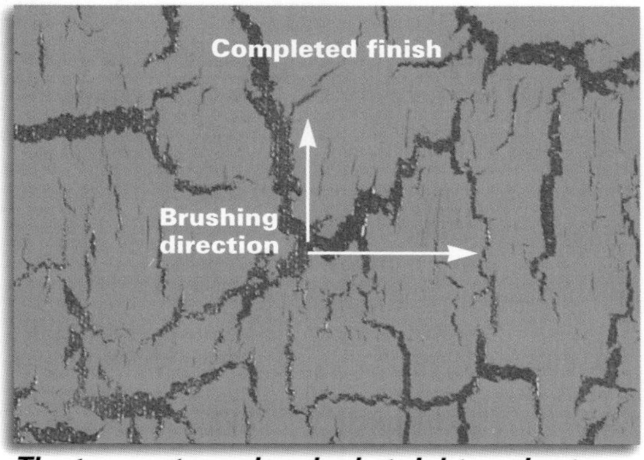

The top coat was brushed at right angles to make this crackle pattern.

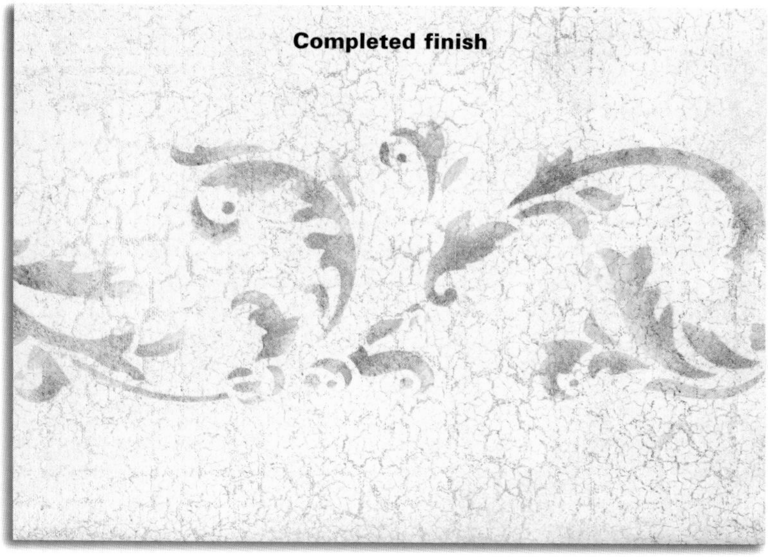

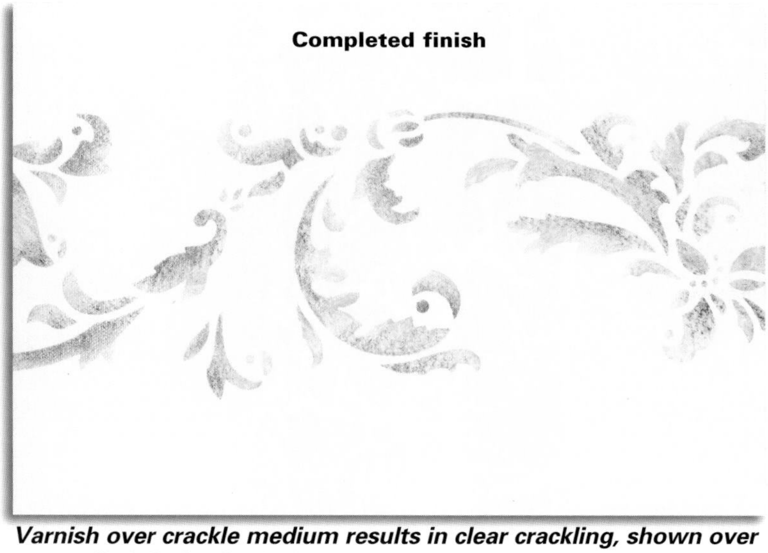

Varnish over crackle medium results in clear crackling, shown over a stenciled design in the bottom photo. To enhance the aged look, rub antiquing glaze into the clear crackles, as shown in progress in the center photo and completed in the top photo.

DISTRESSING

LEVEL

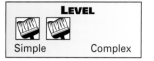

Simple — Complex

SUPPLIES

- Latex paint
- Wax or paraffin
- Base-coating brush
- Metal scraper
- Medium and coarse sandpaper

Distressing makes surfaces look worn. The technique is easy to do using wax and paint. Antiquing medium is sometimes used as well.

Distressed finishes can be made with either one or two colors of paint. When using one color, the natural color of the wood becomes the base color. When using two paint colors, the base-coat color will be mostly hidden under the second color.

When using the natural surface for your base, rub wax or paraffin on parts of the surface, going with the grain of the wood. Concentrate on areas where paint would most likely be worn by handling—along edges and around knobs and pulls, for example. The wax keeps paint from adhering to these areas. This technique is called *wax resist.*

For a two-color finish, base-coat the surface and let it dry. Then rub wax onto the wear areas as described above.

PROCEDURE: Apply one to three coats of the finish color for good coverage. Let it dry between coats, but do not sand between coats. Scrape the dry paint with a metal scraper, working in the direction of the wood grain. In areas where the wax was applied, the paint will flake off easily. Brush away the paint particles as you scrape.

To enhance the effect, remove additional paint with coarse sandpaper, then smooth with fine sandpaper. Distress the surface further by making dings and dents, wormholes, or scratches with knives, hammers, screwdrivers, awls, and other tools.

Antiquing the distressed surface gives the paint a faded appearance and ages the wood that shows under the paint. To antique the finish, mix equal parts of glazing medium and brown paint for your antiquing medium. You can use premixed mediums or wood stains. Be sure you sand off all the wax or the antiquing medium will not work.

WORKS WONDERS ON...

Distressed finishes are ideal for small items and furniture, where it's effective on edges of tabletops. This kind of finish works well on woodwork, such as mantels, windowsills, and built-in cabinetry.

Black paint over unfinished wood, antiqued with reddish-brown glaze.

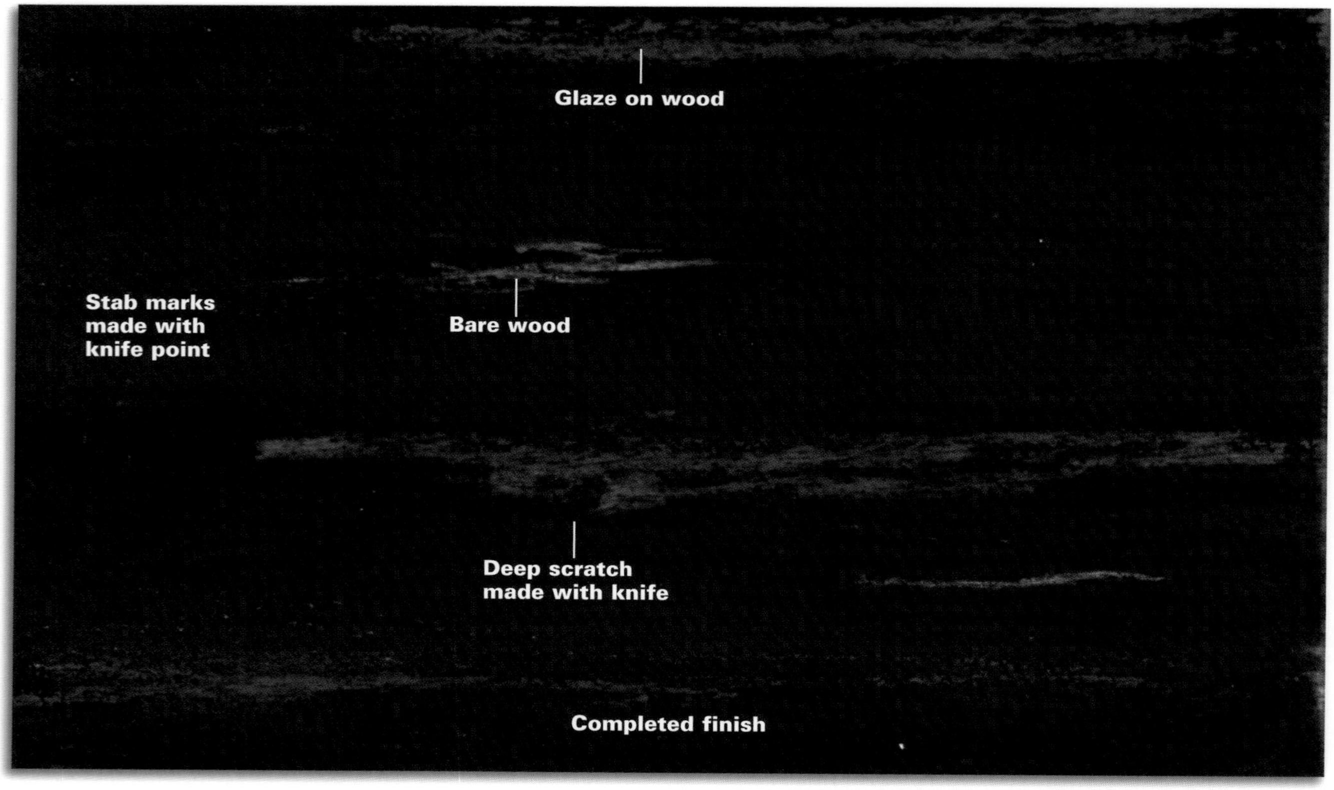

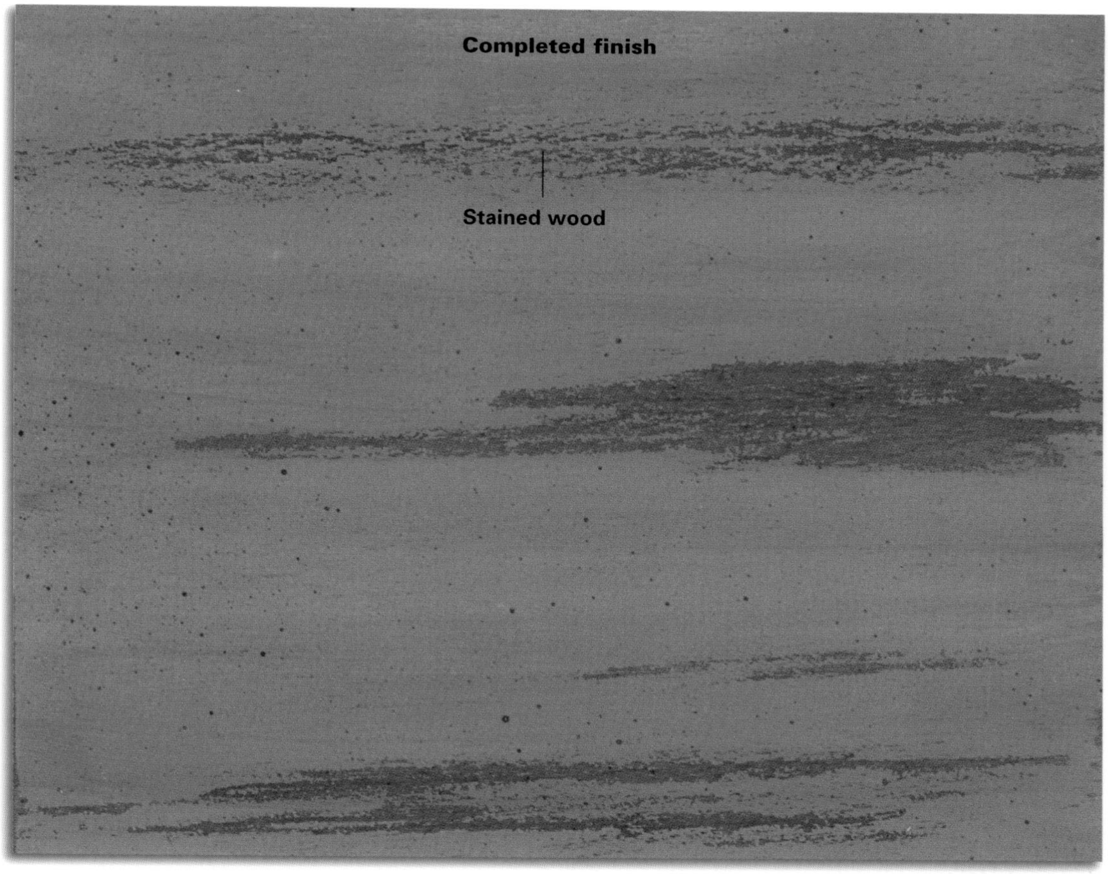

Brown paint and dark brown spattering (see page 76) over wood with mahogany stain.

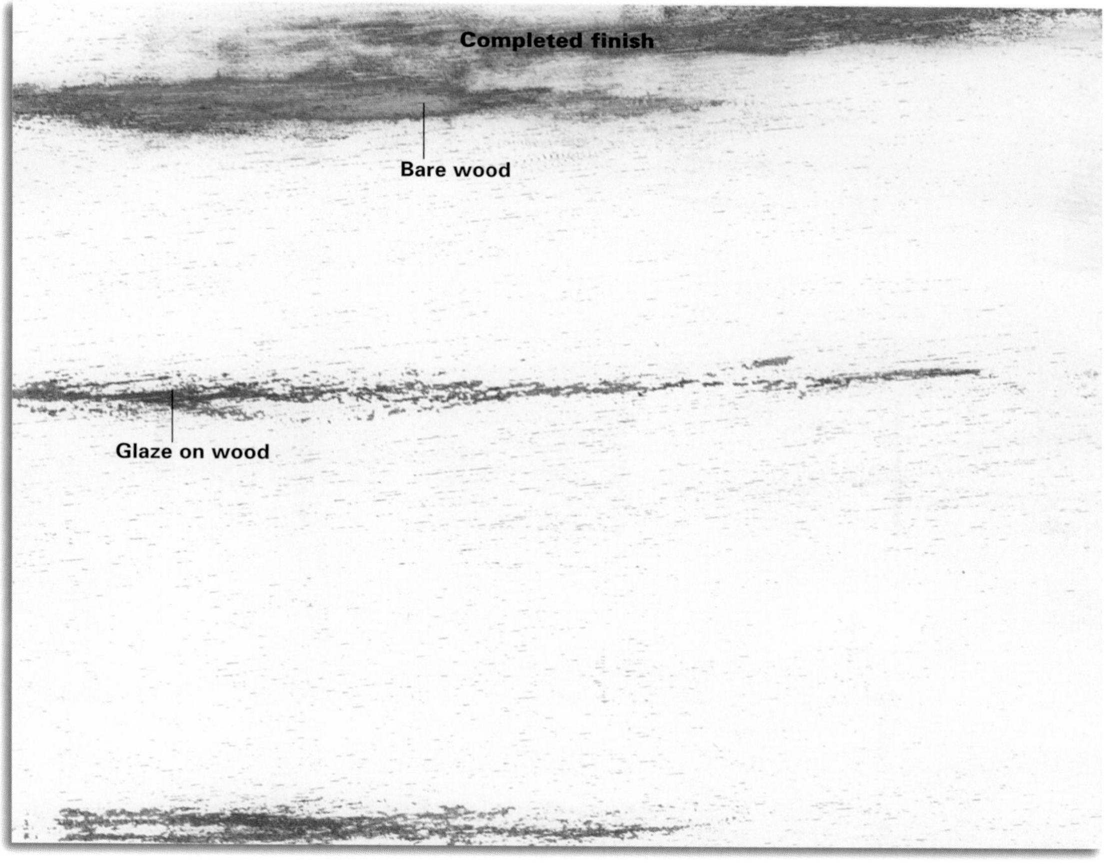

Ivory paint over unfinished wood, antiqued with brown glaze.

DRAGGING

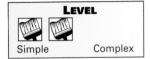

LEVEL

Simple Complex

SUPPLIES

- Latex paint
- Tinted glaze
- Dragging brush
- Cellulose sponge

Dragging—pulling a stiff bristle brush through the glaze—makes a pattern of fine, closely spaced lines. Pulling the edge of a damp cellulose sponge through the wet glaze gives similar results.

On tight curves or edges, you may have to use both tools to create a softly streaked appearance.

PROCEDURE: Prepare the surface and apply a base coat of latex wall paint. For the best overall effect, make the base coat as smooth as possible. Apply one or two coats, and allow the base coat to dry completely.

Mix the glaze color. Use water-base glaze over latex paint. Mix the top paint color 50-50 with neutral glaze base. A top color similar to the base color works well. You can add more glaze base to produce the tint you want.

Apply the glaze with a brush, pad, or roller. Make a smooth, even application, covering only as much area as you can work before the glaze dries.

Work the glaze with the dragging brush. Pull the brush through the glaze in one continuous stroke, holding the brush at an angle to the surface with the bristles trailing. As you begin the next stroke, overlap the edge of the previous one slightly to avoid a ridge. Always drag in the same direction. Clean the bristles with a moist rag or towel after each stroke to keep glaze from building up and drying in the brush. Glaze buildup would change the dragging texture.

You can drag with a cellulose sponge too. Moisten the sponge, then drag an edge of it through the glaze. Don't hold a face of the sponge flat against the surface. Wipe excess glaze from the sponge to avoid buildup.

Buy a special dragging brush (the one with the blue handle) or make one by cutting away the outside bristles on an inexpensive 4-inch, synthetic-bristle paintbrush.

Maintain even pressure on the brush as you pull it through the wet glaze. A damp cellulose sponge will also work.

WORKS WONDERS ON...

Dragging, sometimes called striating, adds texture to a surface and works well on walls. The technique is used to create finishes that imitate the look of silk, denim, linen, or other fabrics.

Completed finish

Dragging creates a fine, linear texture that is often used to represent fabric. This example shows a gold-color glaze over a yellow base coat.

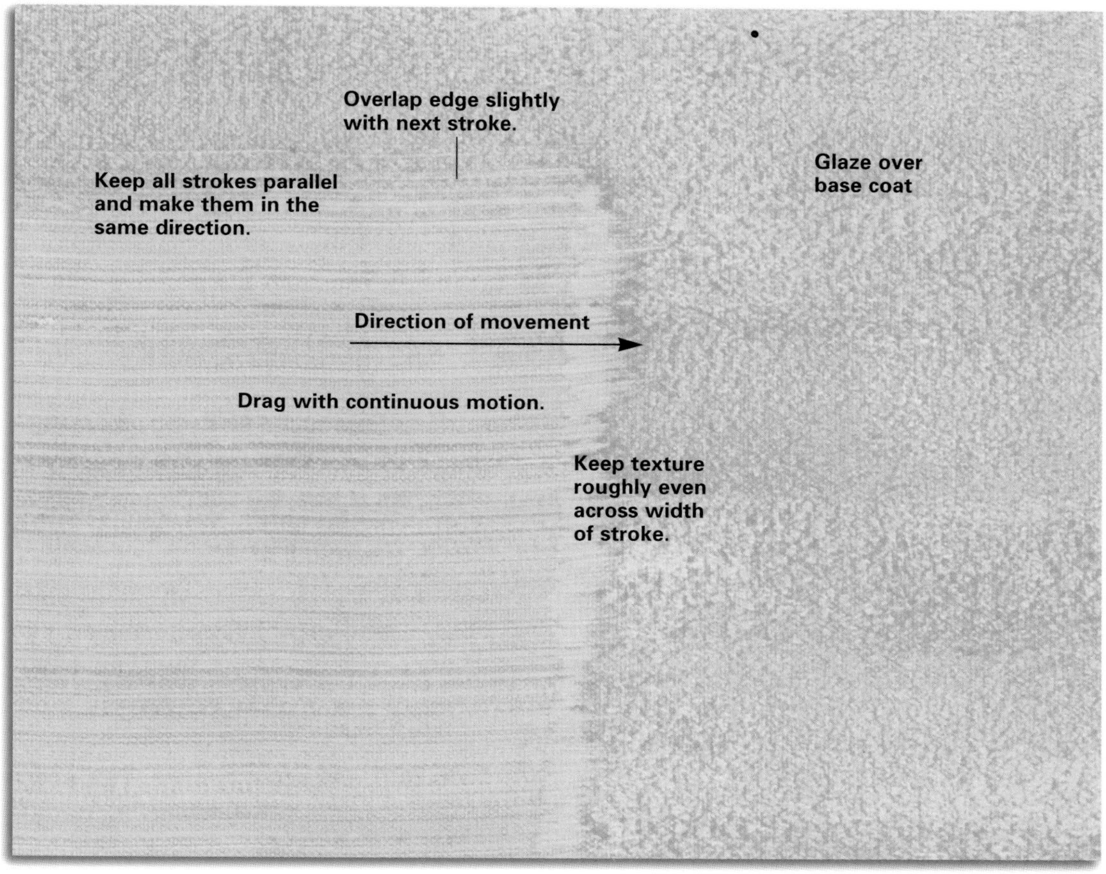
Overlap edge slightly with next stroke.
Glaze over base coat
Keep all strokes parallel and make them in the same direction.
Direction of movement
Drag with continuous motion.
Keep texture roughly even across width of stroke.

FLOGGING

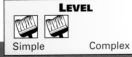

LEVEL

Simple Complex

Slap the bristles of the flogging brush flat against the surface, but don't let the ferrule hit. Overlap the strokes for a continuous texture.

Flogging textures a glazed surface with densely packed streaks. The flogging finish is created by slapping the wet glaze surface with a special brush that has long, floppy bristles. (A house painting brush with natural bristles will work too.) Flogging is particularly effective on a glaze that has random light and dark streaks.

Only the glaze that sticks to the brush bristles is removed. The base coat is completely covered.

PROCEDURE: Prepare the surface, and apply one or two coats of satin or eggshell wall paint. Allow the base coat to dry at least 24 hours before applying the glaze coat.

Mix the glaze color. Blend your choice of paint color (water-base) with a neutral water-base glaze. A 50-50 mix of paint to neutral glaze works well. You can mix additional neutral glaze into the paint for a more translucent effect; the more glaze, the lighter the color tint. (You can use oil-base paints and neutral glaze, if you prefer. The procedures are the same.)

Apply the glaze to the surface evenly with a brush, pad, or roller. Work in small areas or have someone help so you can work the glaze before it dries or sets up.

While the glaze is still wet, flog it with the brush. Slap the surface with the side of the long bristles so the bristles press into the wet glaze and leave a series of fine lines. Work from the bottom of the surface up, holding the brush either vertically or horizontally, depending on which way you want the lines to run. An interlocked woven pattern comes from alternating the brush orientation. Working vertically—one brush width at a time—is a standard pattern.

Repeatedly flog the bristles against the surface. Wipe and clean the bristles periodically with a soft, damp cloth. This prevents any glaze buildup on the bristles that could alter the pattern.

After completing one brush-width row, move to the bottom edge of the next row and repeat the process.

If you want to add light streaks in certain areas, drag cheesecloth through the flogged glaze, then flog those areas again.

Repeat the process of applying glaze, flogging vertical rows bottom to top, adding light streaks, and continuing on to adjacent rows until the entire surface is completed.

SUPPLIES

- Flogging brush or natural-bristle house painting brush
- Glazing medium
- Cheesecloth

WORKS WONDERS ON...

Flogging is a good treatment for walls and other large surfaces. It adds visual texture. It is often used for wood graining to create dense streaking in the grain.

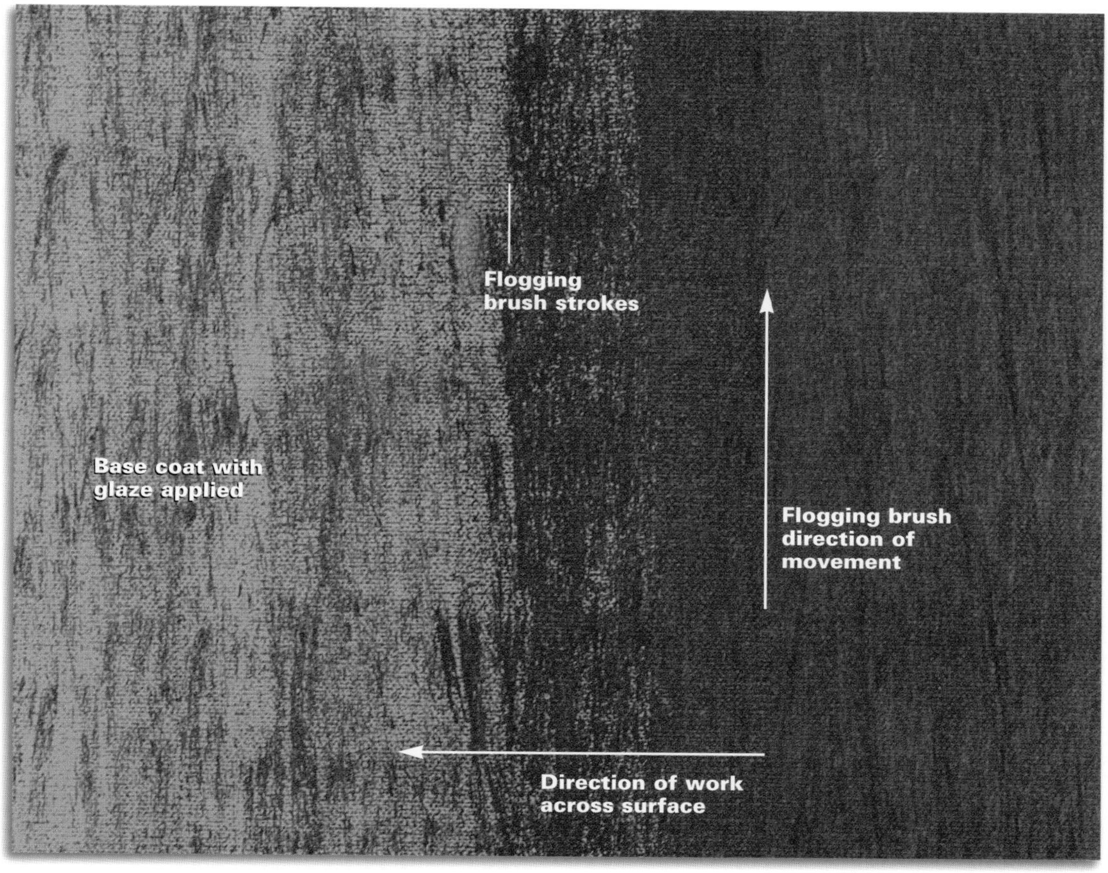

Flogging leaves a finely textured surface. You can combine flogging with other decorative paint techniques.

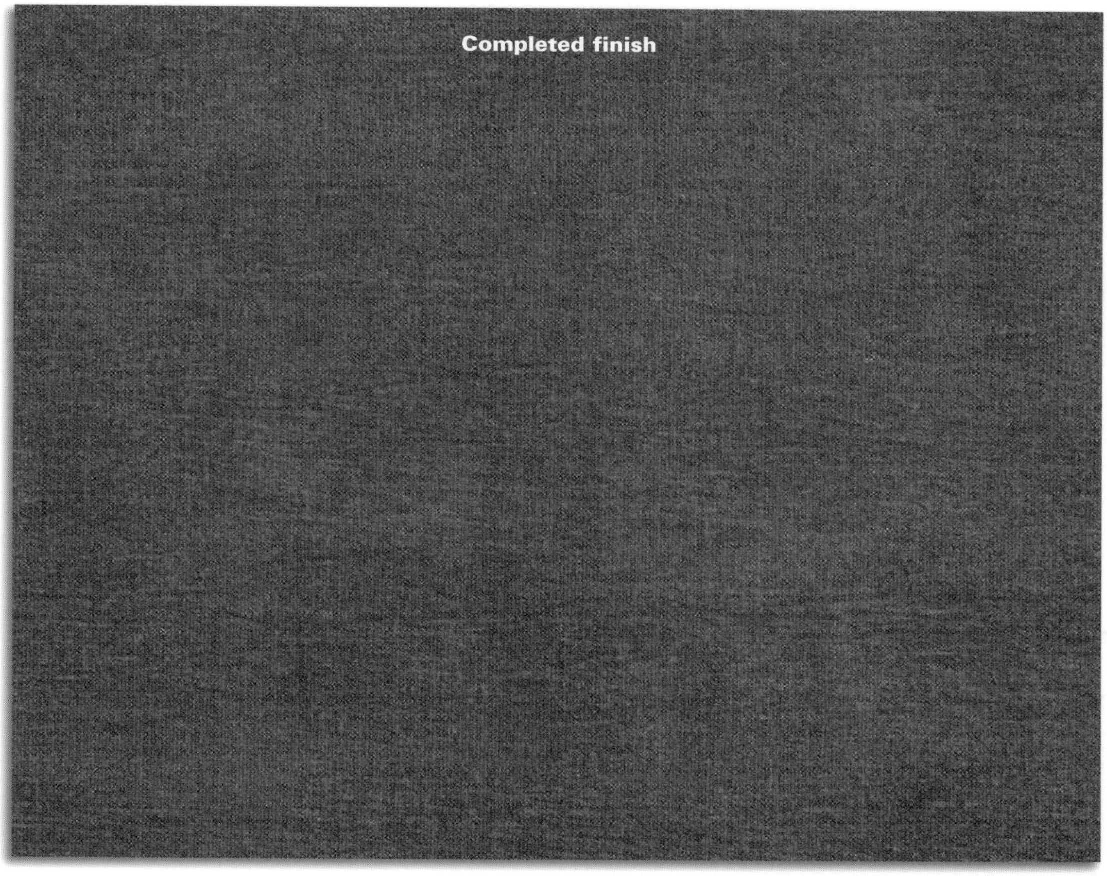

GOLD LEAFING

LEVEL

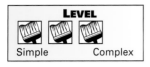

Simple Complex

SUPPLIES

- Gold leaf sizing
- Composition gold leaf
- Paint for base coat
- Acrylic varnish
- Paintbrushes
- Rags
- Sealer for bare wood

Gold leafing is a brilliant and elegant accent that suits a variety of items. Gold leafing—or gilding—often decorates furniture, picture and mirror frames, and small boxes and accessories.

The technique originated many centuries ago, and used to require the painstaking application of thin slivers of gold to surfaces ranging from ornate picture frames to cathedral domes.

Today's leafing materials are not pure gold, but a combination of metals that give the look of gold without the expense.

For gold leafing, you'll need composition gold leaf (other metals are available too; the process for applying them is the same) and some leaf sizing—the liquid adhesive that bonds the leaf to the surface. You'll also need a variety of brushes, acrylic paints, transparent tape, clean cotton rags, and high-quality acrylic varnish. Art supply stores, crafts stores, and many home centers sell these materials. Kits usually include about 25 delicate leaves of composition gold leaf, each roughly 5 inches square.

Gold leafing shows up any imperfections on the base surface, so make sure your workpiece is smooth. Fill holes in wood and sand the surface with 150- and 220-grit sandpapers.

PROCEDURE: Apply a sealer to bare wood. Make sure the workpiece is dry and dust-free.

Base-coat areas to be gilded with a mid-to-dark-value acrylic paint. Let dry. Then lightly sand the surface to remove any wood grain raised by the paint. Dust the surface with a tack cloth.

For a stripe or an ornamental shape, mask off the area with transparent tape. Next, apply an even coat of gold-leaf adhesive sizing

Gold-leafed lines and medallions accent this small cabinet. The gold leaf has been rubbed away in some places to simulate aging.

WORKS WONDERS ON...

Gold leafing serves best as an accent, applied as stripes, ornamental shapes, or over specific details, rather than as a finish for large surfaces. It makes maximum impact when applied sparingly.

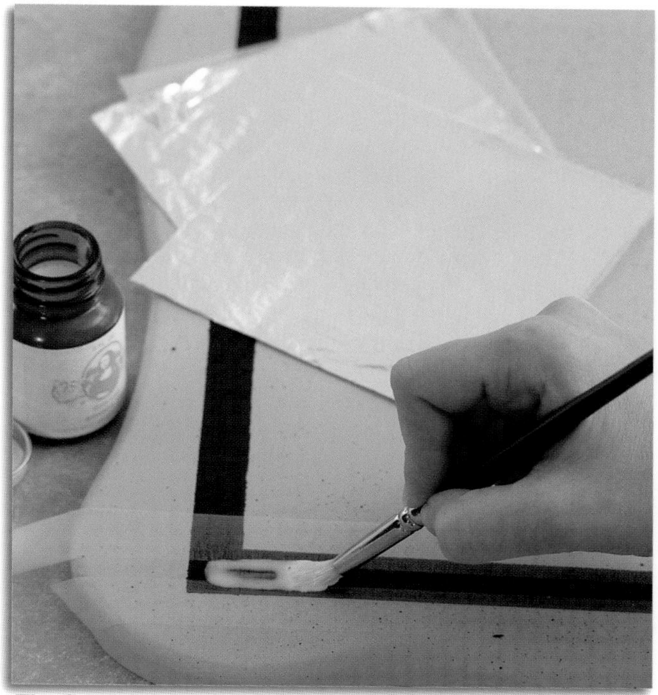

The first step in gold leafing is to brush on the sizing. Here, a stripe has been masked off for gold leafing.

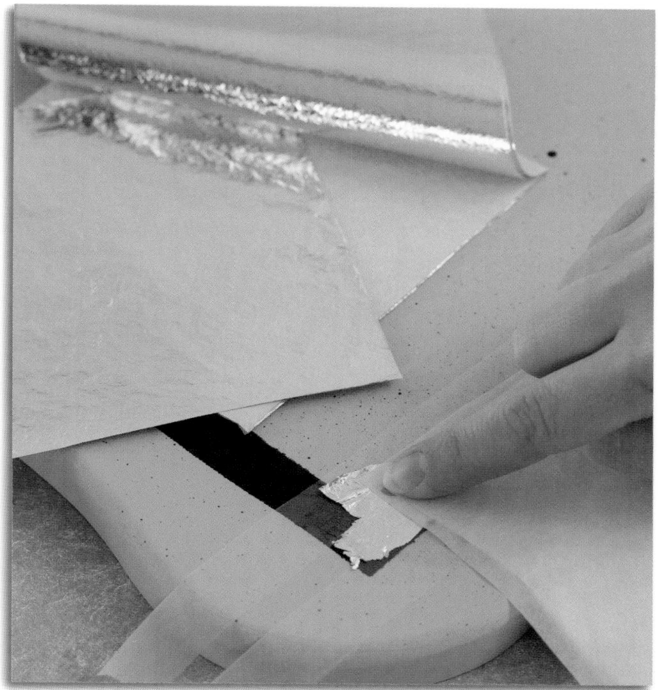

Lay the gold leaf onto the sized surface next. Protect the leaf with tissue as you smooth and press it on.

to the surface. Wash out your brush immediately in warm, soapy water. As the sizing dries (it takes about an hour), it changes from milky white to clear. Once it dries, it remains tacky for about 24 hours.

Handle the gold-leaf material carefully. Don't touch it with your fingers—oil from your hands will tarnish the surface. Work in an area away from air currents because the slightest breeze will blow away the lightweight leaf.

Pick up a leaf of gold, leaving the tissue on top. Place it on the surface quickly to avoid wrinkles. Lightly press over the tissue to adhere the gold to the surface. As you position the leaf, leave gaps between pieces for a worn, antique look, or overlap the pieces for solid coverage. Lift away the tissue and the large pieces of excess leaf. Don't attempt to tear away the tape or the small leaf fragments until the leaf is fully adhered to the sizing.

Slowly remove the tape if you masked an area. Then wipe the surface lightly with a clean rag to remove small flakes of leaf. Seal the surface with two coats of varnish, allowing it to dry between coats. Sealing the surfaces protects the gold leaf from peeling.

For touch up, or to gold-leaf small pieces, rub-on products are available in a tube. These come in a variety of gold tones and can be rubbed on with a paper towel or tissue.

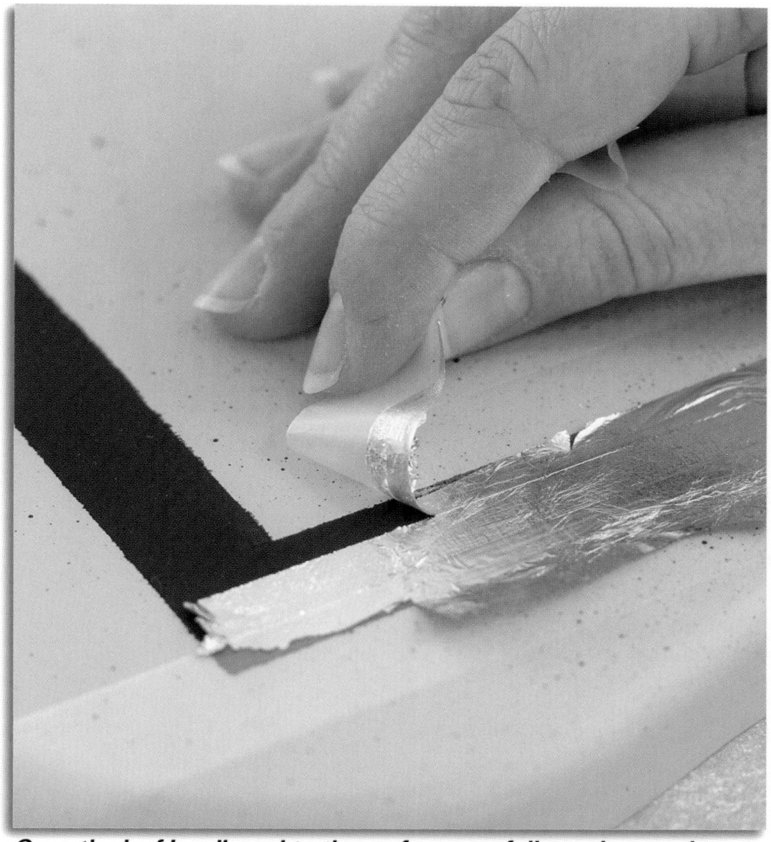

Once the leaf is adhered to the surface, carefully peel away the masking. Seal the surface with varnish to protect the gold leaf.

WOOD GRAINING

LEVEL

Simple — Complex

The face of the graining tool has a series of curved ridges.

To paint a wood grain effect, apply glaze over a base coat, then pull a wood-graining tool through the glaze. Success depends on correct manipulation of the graining tool, so practice the technique on scrap material before you start your project.

PROCEDURE: Start your project by painting on the base color. Let dry. Then with a stippling brush, pounce the dark-tinted glaze onto the surface, covering one large area at a time. Do not cover more area than you can grain before the glaze dries.

While the glaze is still wet, pull the wood-graining tool through the glaze. Rock the tool as you pull, as shown in the photo below. The grain will look better if you pull and rock the tool the entire length of the area you are working before lifting the tool. Wipe excess glaze from the tool with a damp cloth at the end of each pass. Overlap each pass slightly over the edge of the previous one to prevent gaps in the wood graining.

After graining and while the glaze is still wet, flap a flogging brush along the surface (see page 62) to soften the graining and add fine detail lines that enhance the wood look.

SUPPLIES

- Latex house paint
- Clear glaze
- Tinted glaze (burnt umber for wood color)
- Wood-graining tool
- Stippling brush
- Flogging brush
- Damp cloth

WORKS WONDERS ON...

Wood graining is a versatile finish for surfaces ranging from small boxes to wall paneling. Doors and cabinetry are ideal for wood graining, but curved or detailed surfaces such as moldings are difficult to do.

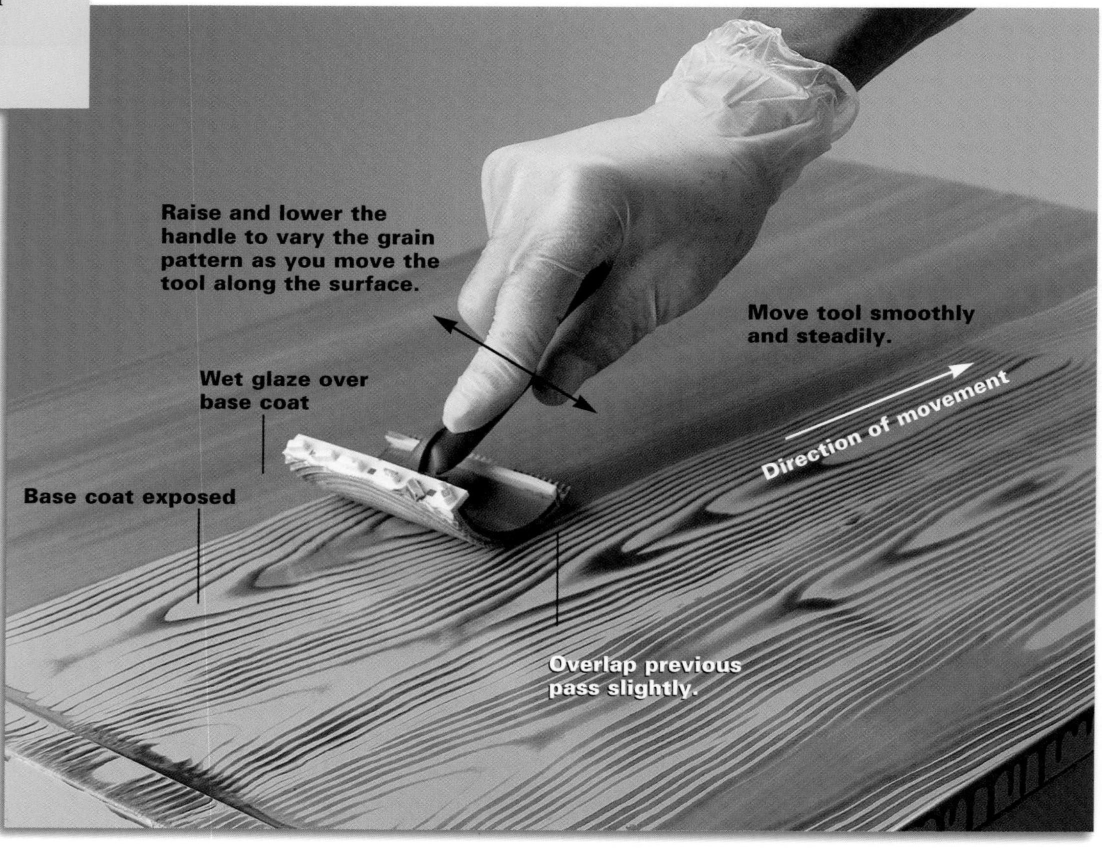
Raise and lower the handle to vary the grain pattern as you move the tool along the surface.
Move tool smoothly and steadily.
Direction of movement
Wet glaze over base coat
Base coat exposed
Overlap previous pass slightly.

Rock the graining tool as you pull it through the glaze. Rocking makes natural-looking variations in the grain pattern. Pull the tool steadily and make a continuous pass; do not lift the tool until you reach the end of the pass.

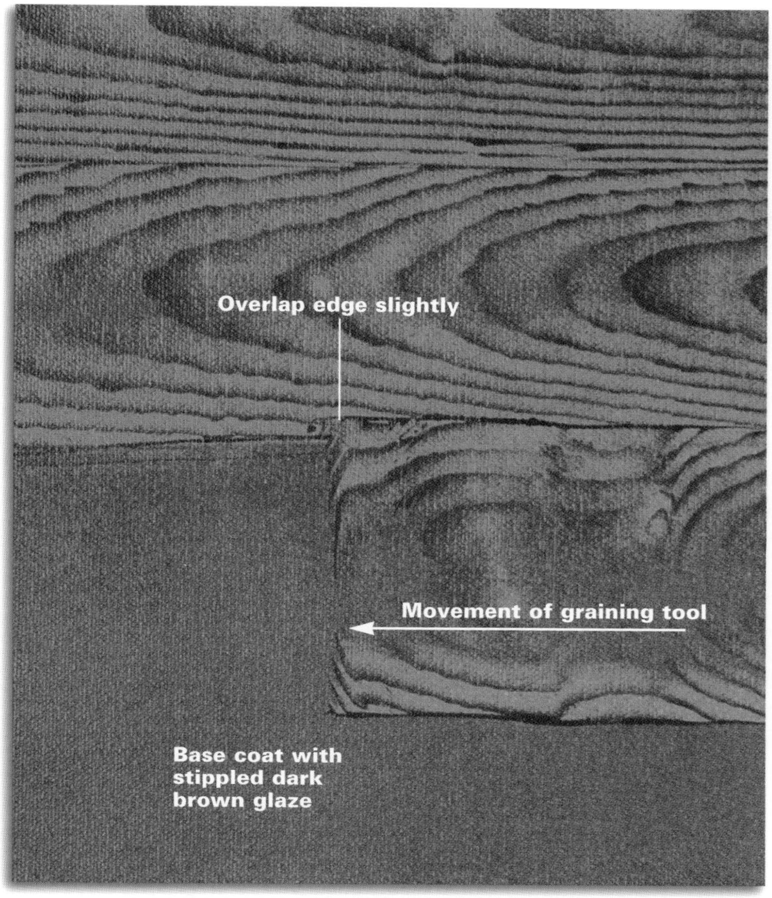

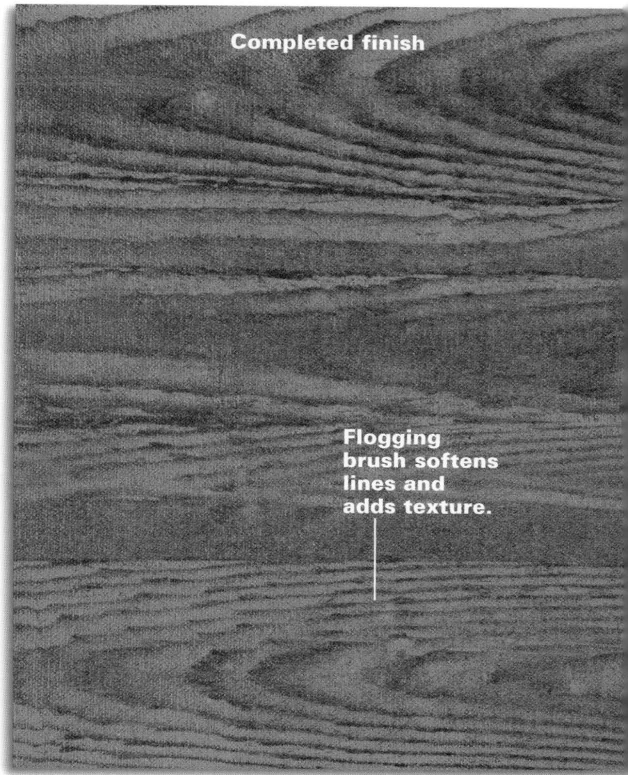

Dark wood grain is made with a dark brown glaze over a dark brown base coat. Too much contrast between the base coat and graining glaze can produce garish results.

Blonde wood grain, reminiscent of pine, is made with a medium brown glaze over a light brown base coat.

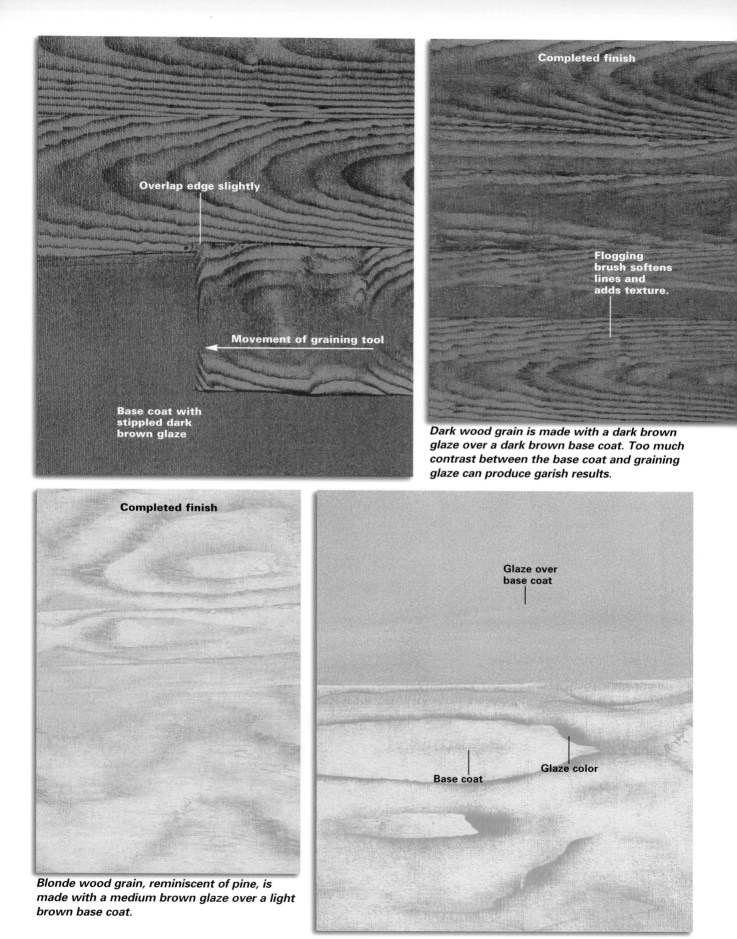

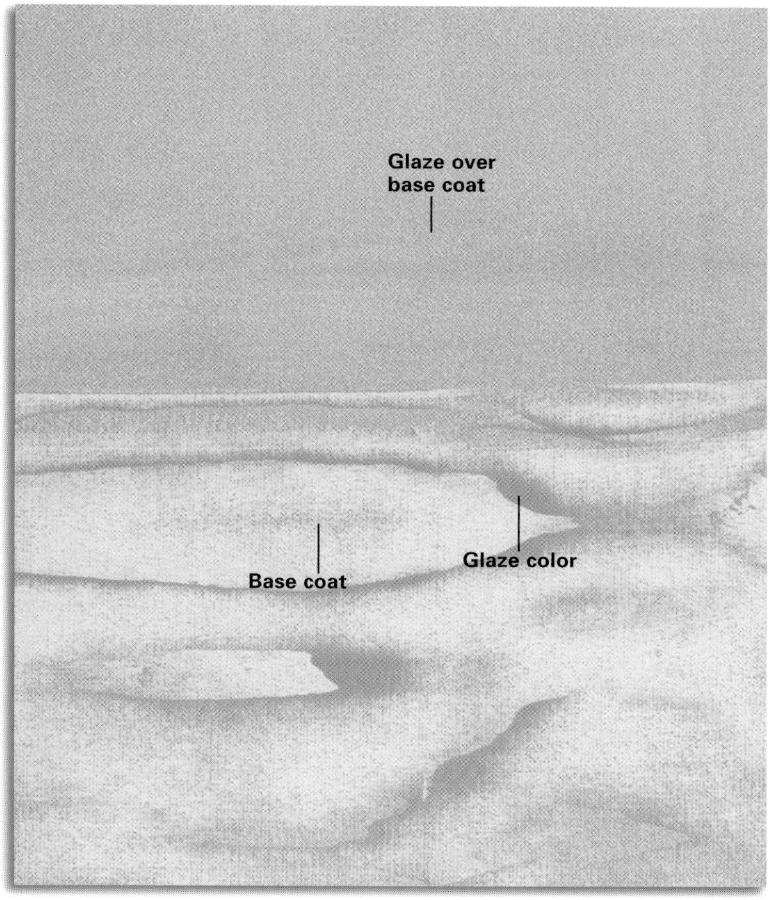

GRANITE

LEVEL

Simple Complex

SUPPLIES

- Latex paint
- Color glazes
- Natural sea sponge

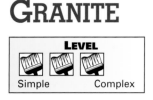

This painted finish imitates the mottled appearance of cut granite. For a glossy surface like polished granite, top it with a gloss clear finish.

PROCEDURE: Prepare the surface and apply one or two coats of satin or eggshell wall paint. Let this base coat dry at least 24 hours before applying the glazes.

To mix the glaze colors, add water-base paint to a neutral water-base glaze. (You can use oil paint and oil-base neutral glaze, if you prefer.) Mix equal amounts of paint and glaze. To lighten the tint and make the glaze more translucent, add more neutral glaze.

Place equal amounts of each glaze color on disposable plates or paint trays. Put one color on each plate.

Moisten a natural sea sponge to make it soft. Lightly pat the sponge face into one of the color glazes. Then pat it into each of the other colors. When you dip the face of the sponge into the paint colors, make sure you don't saturate the sponge—just apply a thin layer of each of the colors randomly. Pick up roughly equal amounts of each color on the sponge. Granite should look tweedy; keeping the colors even on the sponge will prevent a splotchy appearance.

Pat the sponge onto a clean paper plate or a piece of poster board to check the color distribution and pattern. Then, lightly pat it repeatedly on the base-coated surface. Add more glaze to the sponge as needed.

Rinse the sponge periodically so it doesn't become saturated with colors or overworked. Allowing the colors to mix on the sponge will result in a one-color appearance on your project instead of a random multicolor finish.

WORKS WONDERS ON...

Granite is a great faux finish for top surfaces—tabletops and countertops, for instance—and small accessories. It works well on mantelpieces, columns, and other architectural features.

A sponge loaded with the highlight colors makes the random pattern. Keep the colors about equal on the surface of the sponge to create the proper effect.

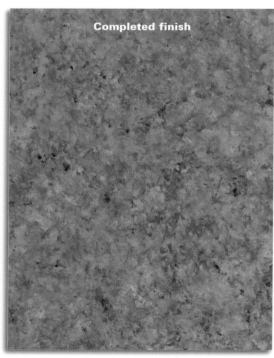

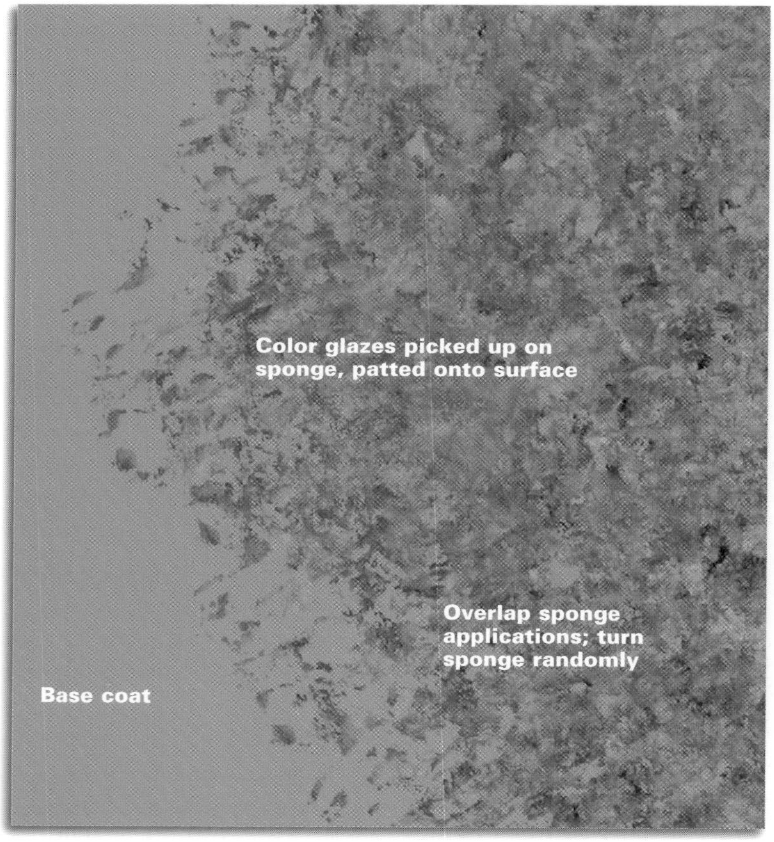
Color glazes picked up on sponge, patted onto surface
Overlap sponge applications; turn sponge randomly
Base coat

Completed finish

Light, medium and dark blue over a medium blue base give a good granite look.

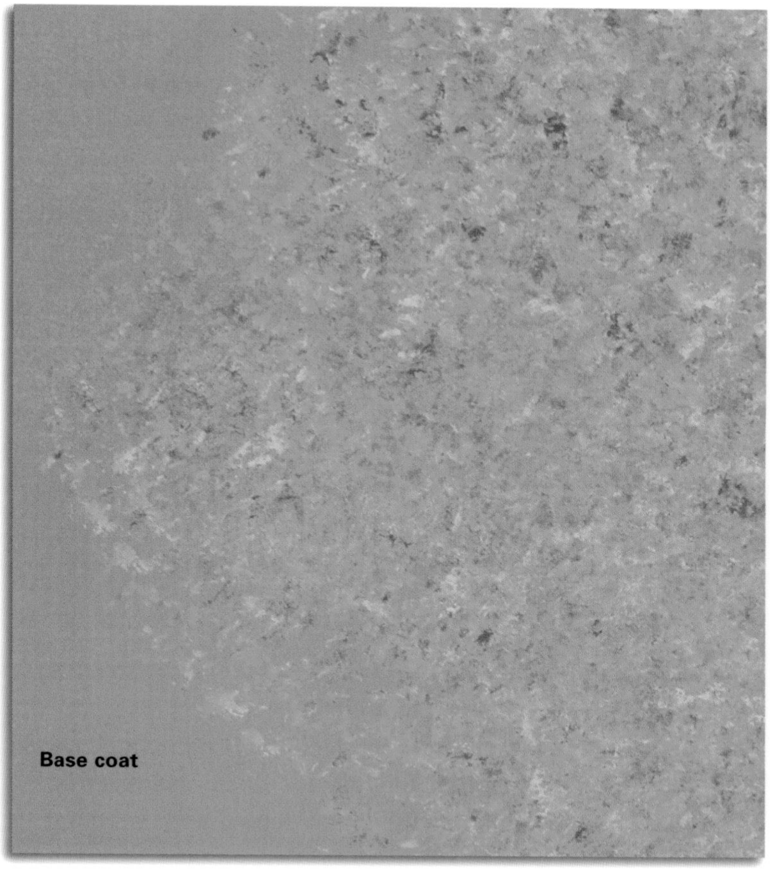

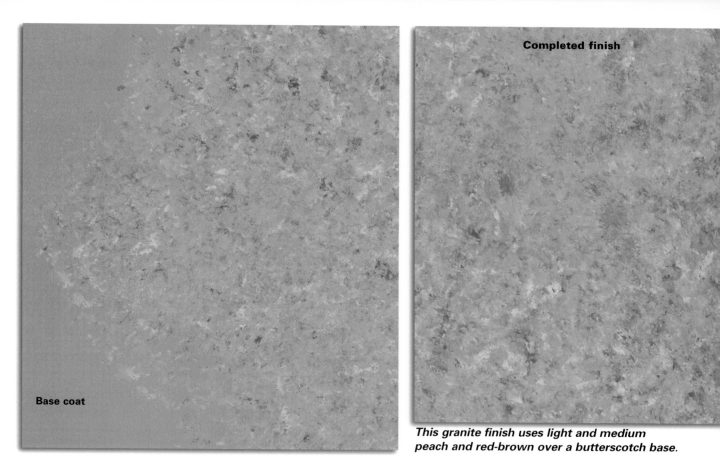

This granite finish uses light and medium peach and red-brown over a butterscotch base.

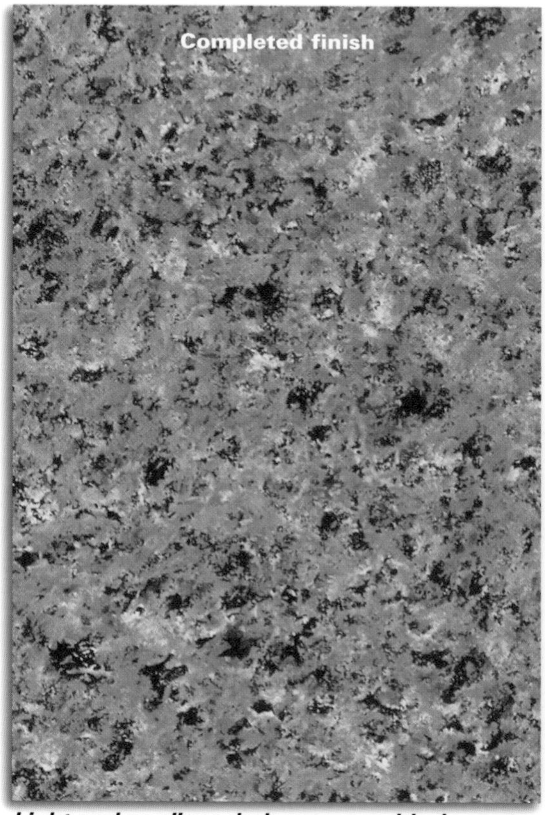

Light and medium-dark gray over black create this traditional-looking granite finish.

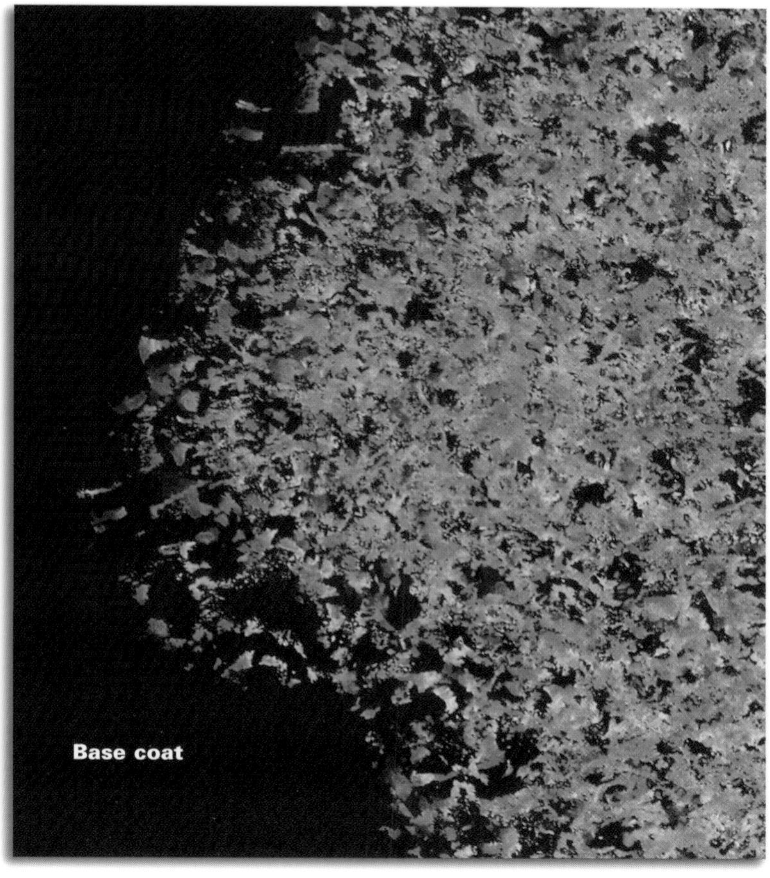

MALACHITE

LEVEL

Simple Complex

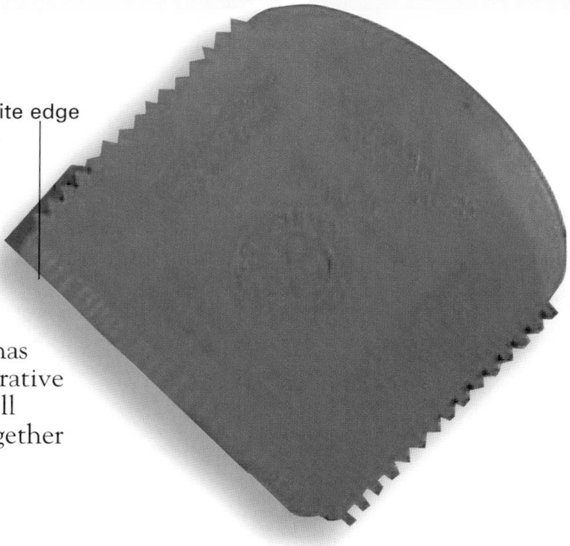

Malachite is a precious stone mined mainly in Russia. The mineral's distinctive grain has long made it a favorite material for decorative artifacts. Because it's rare, chips and small chunks of the stone are often pressed together to form larger pieces, called chunked malachite.

Malachite is a favorite of many faux-finishers too. A combing tool with one edge designed to create the stone's exotic grain is available from art and crafts supply stores and many home centers. Another technique uses paper to create the chunked malachite finish, which looks like small pieces of the stone pressed together.

SUPPLIES

- Medium green paint
- Dark green glaze
- Stippling brush
- Comb with malachite edge
- Copier paper

CHUNKED MALACHITE

Paint the surface with the base coat and mix the glaze as explained for malachite stone. Apply the glaze with a brush or roller. Brush marks aren't a problem with this technique.

While the glaze is still wet, crumple a piece of copier paper into a ball. Press and pounce the wadded paper over the glaze to create the chunked texture. Repeat over the entire surface, changing to a fresh piece of paper whenever the paper softens or becomes soaked with glaze.

Chunked malachite can be used as a complementary technique or by itself. You can quickly pat the surface with the balled-up paper, then comb the glaze so any uncombed surface will show the chunked texture through the pattern design.

MALACHITE STONE

Paint the surface with one or two coats of medium green satin or eggshell paint. This base coat will be exposed by the graining. Roll it on or brush it and stipple it to give a uniform texture. Allow the base coat to dry before applying the colored glaze.

Mix the dark green glaze. A dark forest green—almost black—gives the best effect. You can use either oil paint and oil-base neutral glaze or acrylic paint and water-base

This finish looks like chunked malachite—a piece formed by pressing small chips together.

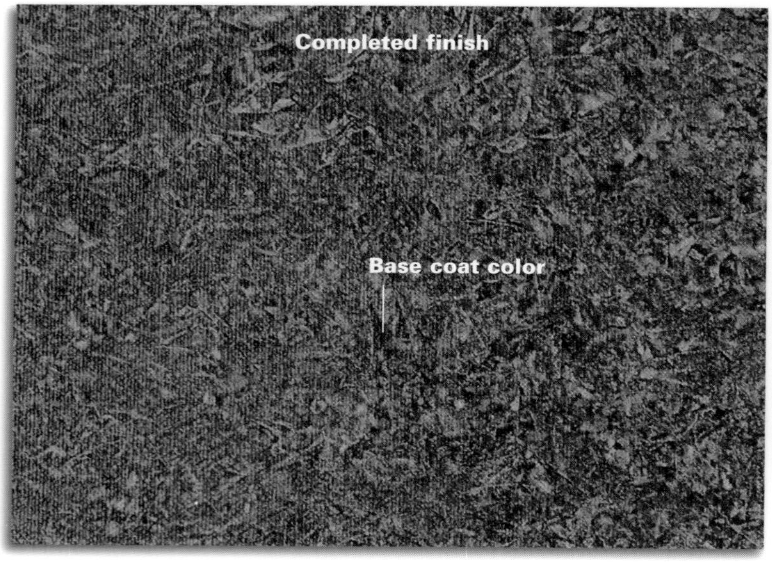

Turn the crumpled paper ball to vary the pattern as you pounce the wet glaze. When glaze builds up on the paper, use a new sheet.

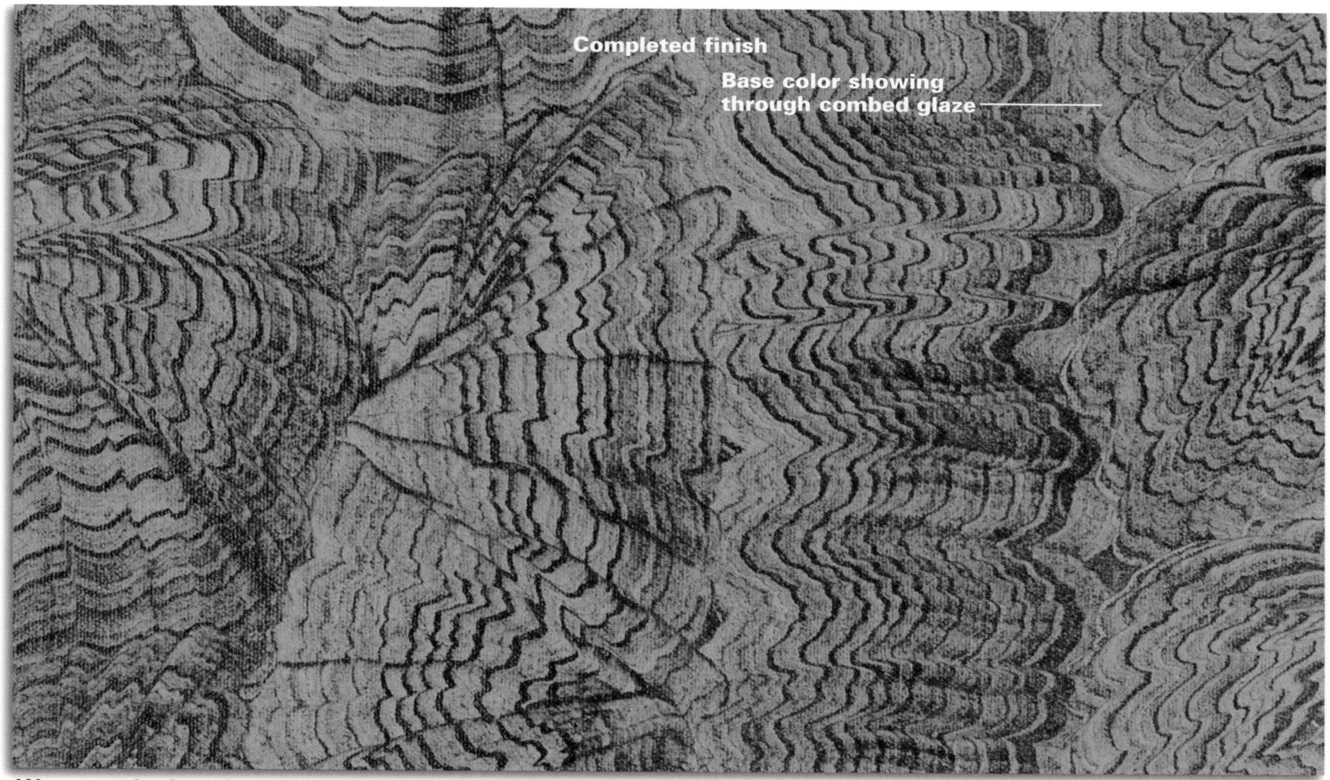

Wavy combed tracks create the distinctive malachite stone pattern.

neutral glaze to mix the glaze. Mix the color and neutral glaze in equal parts.

Roll or brush the color glaze onto the surface, smoothing the color out evenly. Glaze only as much area as you can comb before the glaze dries. If you brush on the glaze coat, go over it with a stippling brush (see page 82) to remove brush marks.

Comb through the glaze with the malachite edge of the tool, creating arcs and waves. (Refer to the photograph above for characteristic pattern designs and shapes.) Remove glaze buildup from the edge of the comb each time you pull it through the glaze by wiping the tool edge with a damp cloth.

Continue glazing and combing the surface until it has been worked completely. You can overlap comb patterns or work next to the previous pattern.

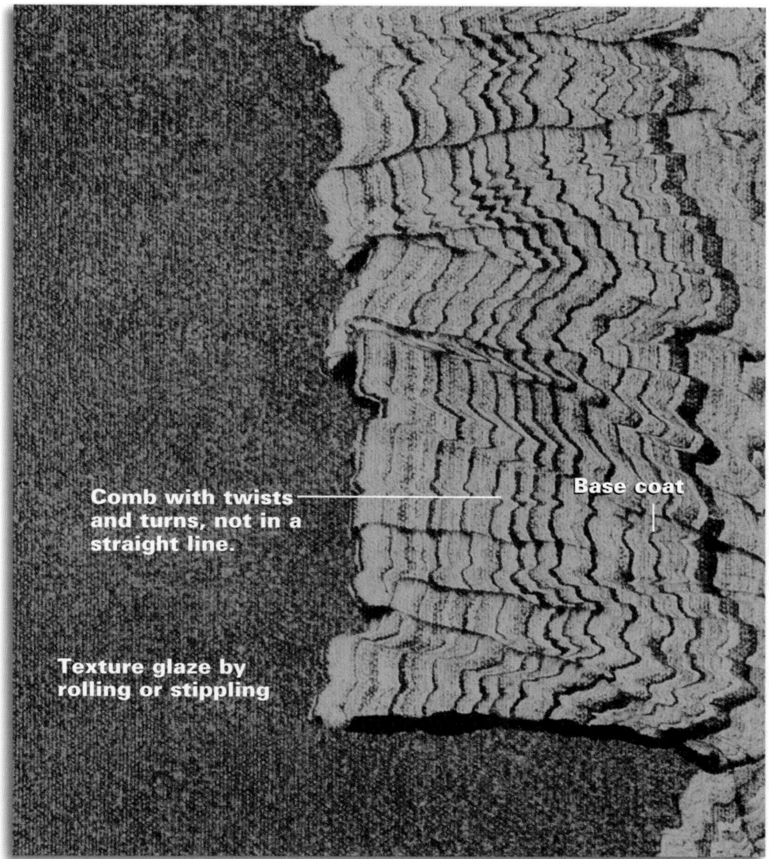

The malachite edge on the comb wipes parallel tracks in the wet glaze. You can let the pattern run wild in arcs and curves.

WORKS WONDERS ON...

Malachite stone is a bold and showy finish that can be overpowering on large surfaces. It works best as an accent or as a finish for small items such as desk boxes, clocks, and other accessories.

MARBLING

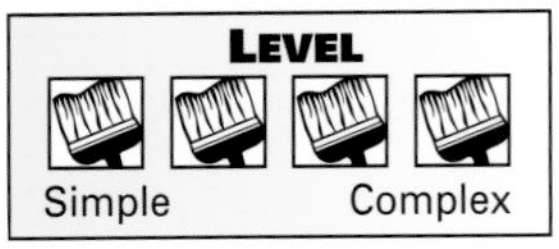

Marbling is a technique first developed to mimic the look of marble. Over time, it has become an art form in its own right; finished work now may either imitate marble or merely suggest it.

Complex formulas for marbling with oil paint date back to the Middle Ages. The simple but traditional technique shown here uses glazes, paint, and mineral spirits. Packaged kits that create marble effects are available too.

SUPPLIES

- Paint
- Glazing liquid
- Wide, soft-bristle brush
- Stippling brush
- Palette plate
- Cellulose sponge
- Feathers
- Spray bottle of water
- Rags for wiping

PROCEDURE: Base-coat the project surface. For the example shown in photos 1–3, the base coat is a black-green color. Let the paint dry thoroughly.

Mix each color with glazing medium. Use a separate container for each color.

Mix medium green for the first marbling color, then mix one part of the medium green with three parts of white for the second color.

Coat the base-coated surface with glazing medium. The medium allows the colors to move as you work with them. Keep a spray bottle of water handy to moisten the surface if it starts to dry out. For this technique, you work with paint on wet paint (wet-on-wet).

Pounce the medium green glazing mixture on some areas of the surface, using a stippling brush and working in a diagonal pattern to create a drift of color. Wipe off the brush with a rag to eliminate any remaining color. Pounce the second color, the light green, onto the surface with the stippling brush. Make sure both colors show distinctly, and allow some of the base-coat color to show through (see photos 1 and 4). When you are pleased with the colors, let the paint dry.

To create the veins, dip a feather tip into white paint. Artist Susan Driggers suggests holding the feather "as a violinist holds a bow." Shake your hand while pulling the feather toward you to paint the veins.

Veins should have wide and narrow areas of color, as shown in photos 2 and 5. Real marble has heavy veining in some areas and no veins in others.

Drag a wide, soft-bristle brush lightly over the white areas to soften the lines and feather out the veins. For the fissure cracks, pull the feather tip through the white paint, then add thin cracks to the painted surface, as shown in photos 3 and 6.

WORKS WONDERS ON...

Marbling is a great way to add character to tabletops, countertops, and similar surfaces. It also works well on mantels, windowsills, and shelves. It looks good on floors, but requires a durable protective coating.

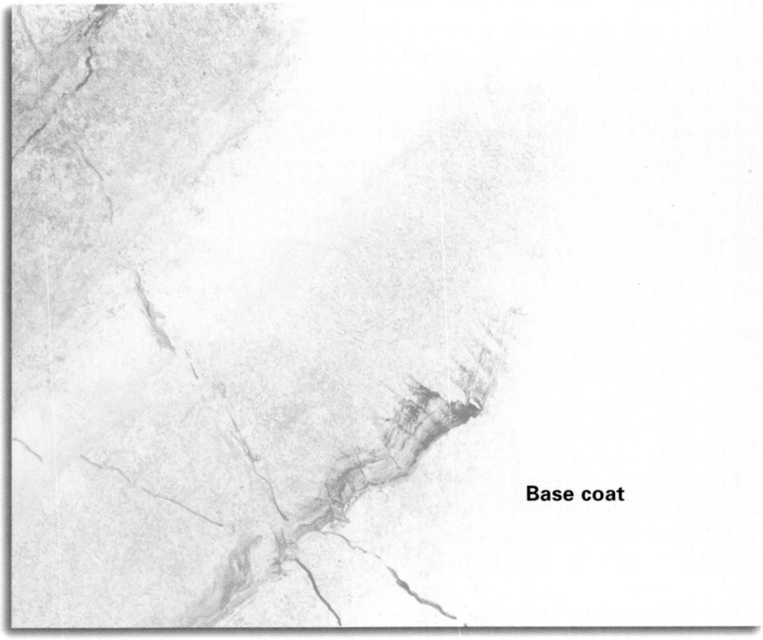

Base coat

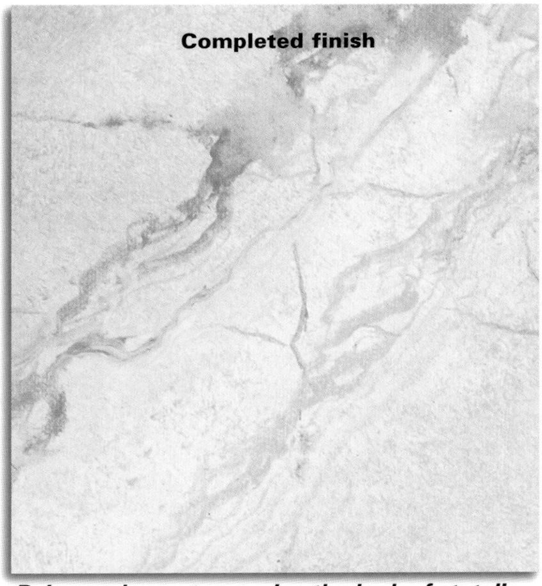

Completed finish

Beige and gray tones give the look of statalia golden vein marble from Italy.

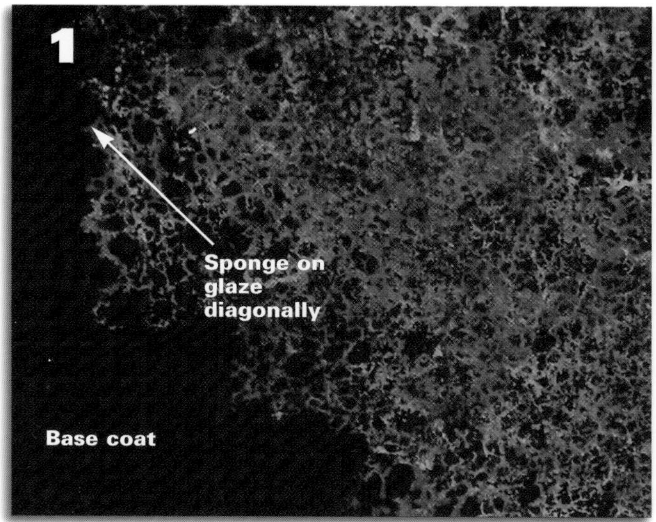

After the base coat dries, pounce the color glazes onto the surface with a stippling brush or a sponge. Work diagonally across the area.

To add veins, dip a feather into white paint and pull the paint across the glazed surface.

Paint white fissure cracks with the feather tip.This pattern resembles Italian verde (green) marble.

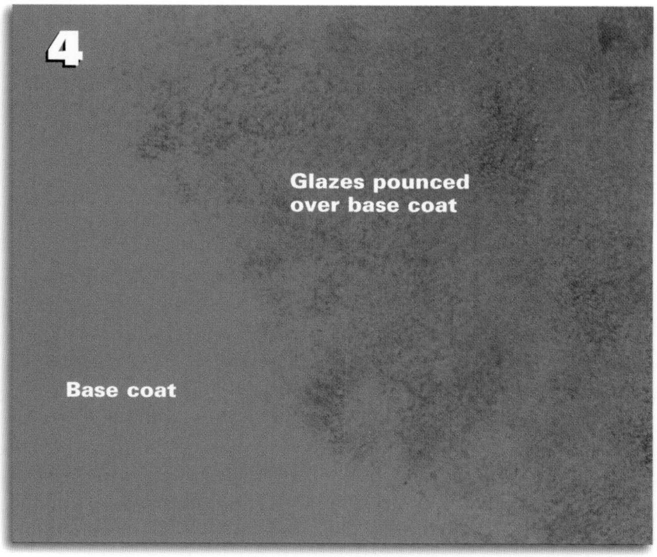

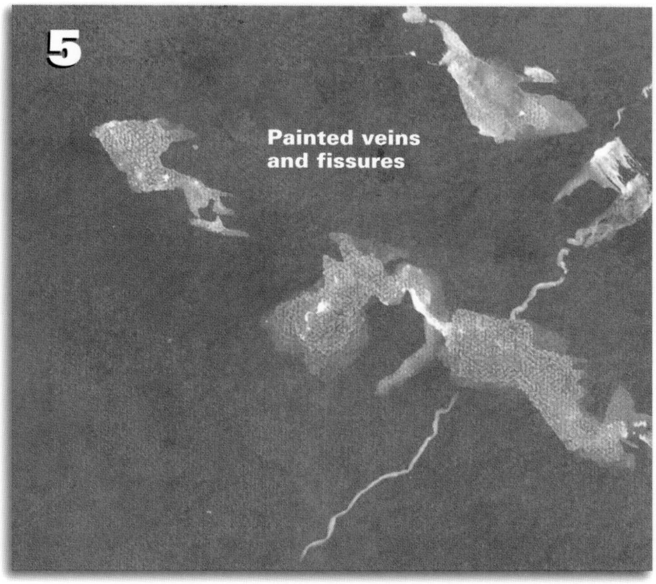

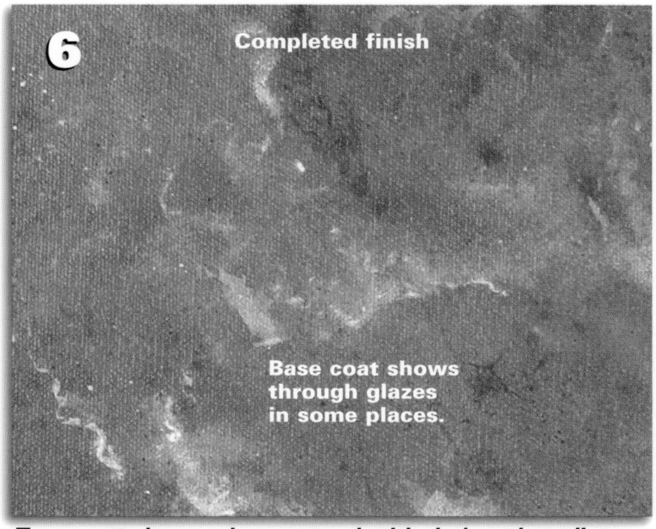

Terra-cotta base color pounced with dark and medium brown glazes gives the look of French rosso merlino marble. Veins are white, beige, and brown.

RAGGING

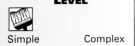

LEVEL

Simple Complex

SUPPLIES

- Neutral glazing medium
- Paint for glaze
- Paint for base coat
- Stirring stick
- Assorted rags, paper, plastic, or ragging mitt

Ragging and rag rolling are simply the application of a glaze over a base coat. The glaze shows the texture of the cloth rags, crumpled paper, plastic, or ragging mitt you use to apply it. Slightly different effects will result from using a rag, paper, or plastic rather than a mitt.

There are two methods for ragging: positive and negative. (See Glazing, page 50.) Positive ragging is the addition of glaze to a base coat, using a rag or mitt as an applicator. Negative ragging is the removal of glaze. In negative ragging, the glaze is painted completely over the base coat. Then, while the glaze is still wet, the rag or mitt is used to blot it off the surface. Wear plastic gloves for either technique.

Practice on a board to determine the colors, method, and ragging material that give the result you want.

PROCEDURE: Start by base-coating the walls or surface with the latex paint color of your choice. Make the surface smooth and uniform. Dark colors may require more coats than light ones.

Mix the ragging color by combining neutral glazing medium with acrylic, oil, or latex paint, depending on the glazing medium. Stir thoroughly with a stirring stick.

Pour the glazing mixture into a paint tray. If you use a mitt for positive ragging, load it by pouncing the face of the mitt into the glaze. Blot the face of the mitt on the grid of the paint tray to distribute the color. If you use a rag, paper, or plastic, dip a piece of the material of a convenient size into the paint to saturate it. Blot it on the grid of the paint pan as you shape it into a roll.

If you use the negative method, brush or roll the glaze onto a section of the wall or surface. Cover only as much area as you can blot with the mitt or rag before the glaze dries. Then remove the glaze by pouncing the dry mitt or rag onto it. Clean or replace the mitt or rag when it loads up with glaze.

Practice will help you learn how much area you can work on at a time, and whether you prefer the rag or mitt method.

WORKS WONDERS ON...

Ragging is a popular wall treatment. You can rag all the walls in a room or highlight a particular area. It can be subtle or dramatic, depending on the colors and the texture left by the application material.

Glaze applied to base coat with ragging mitt.
Base coat

Completed finish

Positive ragging, light glaze over a medium base coat, using a mitt.

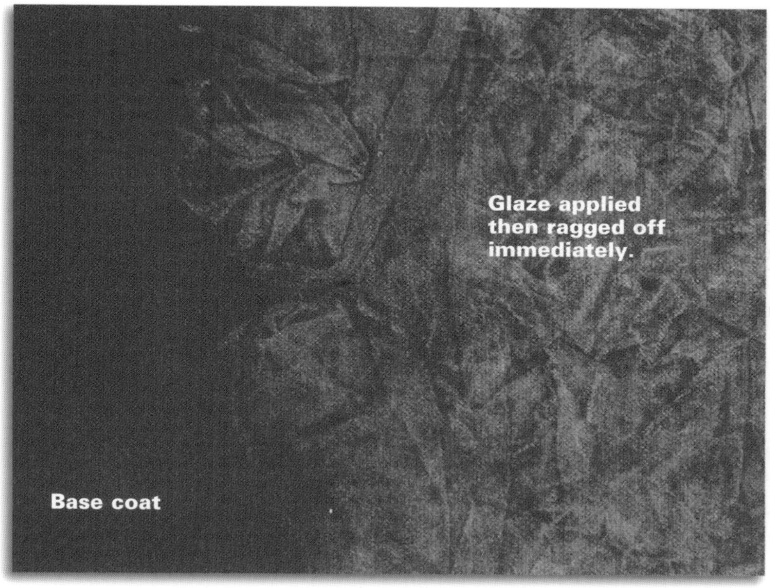
Glaze applied
then ragged off
immediately.
Base coat

Completed finish

Negative ragging, removing light glaze from a dark base coat using a rag.

Completed finish

Positive ragging, dark glaze over medium base coat, using a rag.

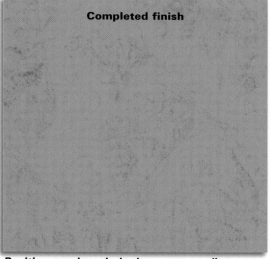

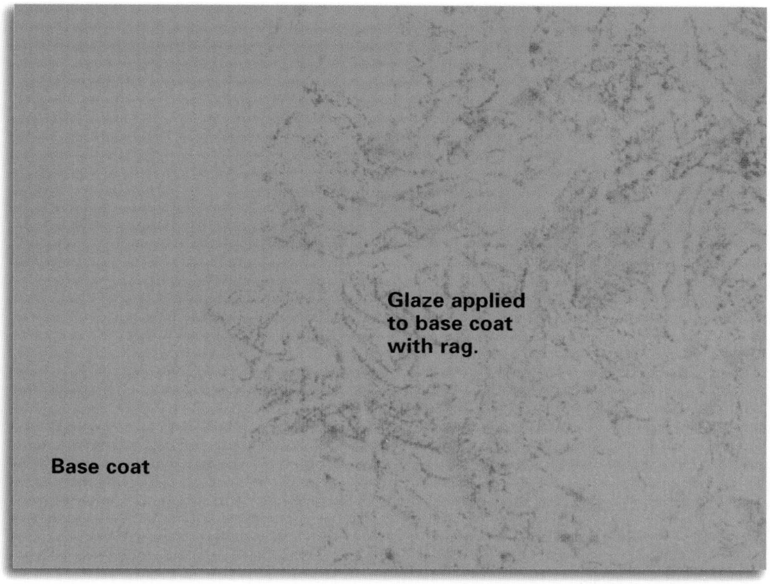
Glaze applied
to base coat
with rag.
Base coat

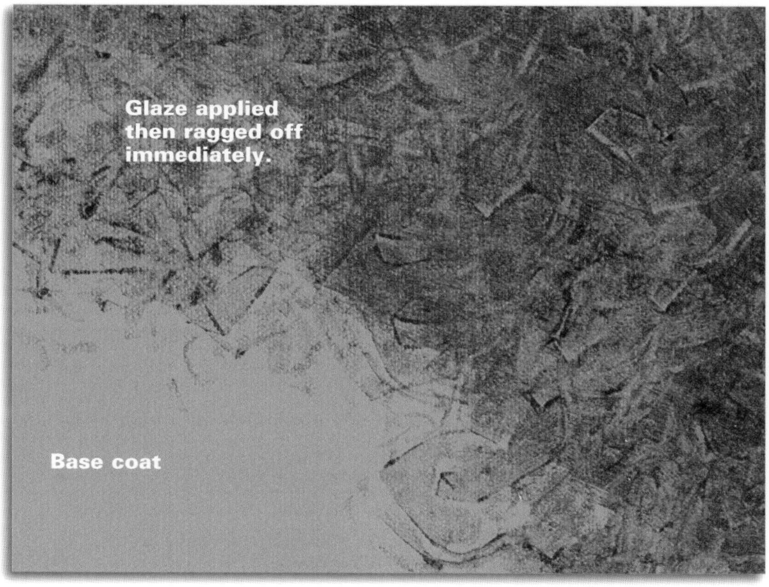
Glaze applied
then ragged off
immediately.
Base coat

Completed finish

Negative ragging, removing dark glaze from a medium base coat, using a mitt.

SPATTERING

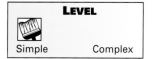

LEVEL
Simple — Complex

SUPPLIES

- Glazing medium
- Acrylic paint
- Spatter tool and brush
- Toothbrush
- Nail brush

Spattering, sometimes called fly-specking, adds a distressed, aged look to a painted or stained surface. The spatters are easy to make with a spatter tool (a mesh screen on a handle) and a brush, or with an old toothbrush, nail brush, or other stiff-bristle brush.

PROCEDURE: For either method, thin the paint to the consistency of ink. Mix glazing medium with oil paints or thin acrylic or latex paint with water. If your specks do not flick from the brush bristles easily, thin the paint a little more.

To spatter with a toothbrush or stiff-bristle brush, dip the bristles into the thinned paint mixture and run your thumb across the bristles to spray or flick the paint in the direction of the project surface. (Protect surrounding areas with paper; your aim may not be accurate.)

To use the spatter tool, dip the tips of the brush bristles in paint, then rub them over the mesh. Drops of paint will spatter on the surface in a manner somewhat different than with a toothbrush. Try both methods to see which look you prefer.

WORKS WONDERS ON...

Spatter black over any finish, such as antiquing or distressing, to add to the aged look. You can spatter over a base color with a darker shade or lighter tint of the same color, another color, or spatter with several hues for a colorful effect.

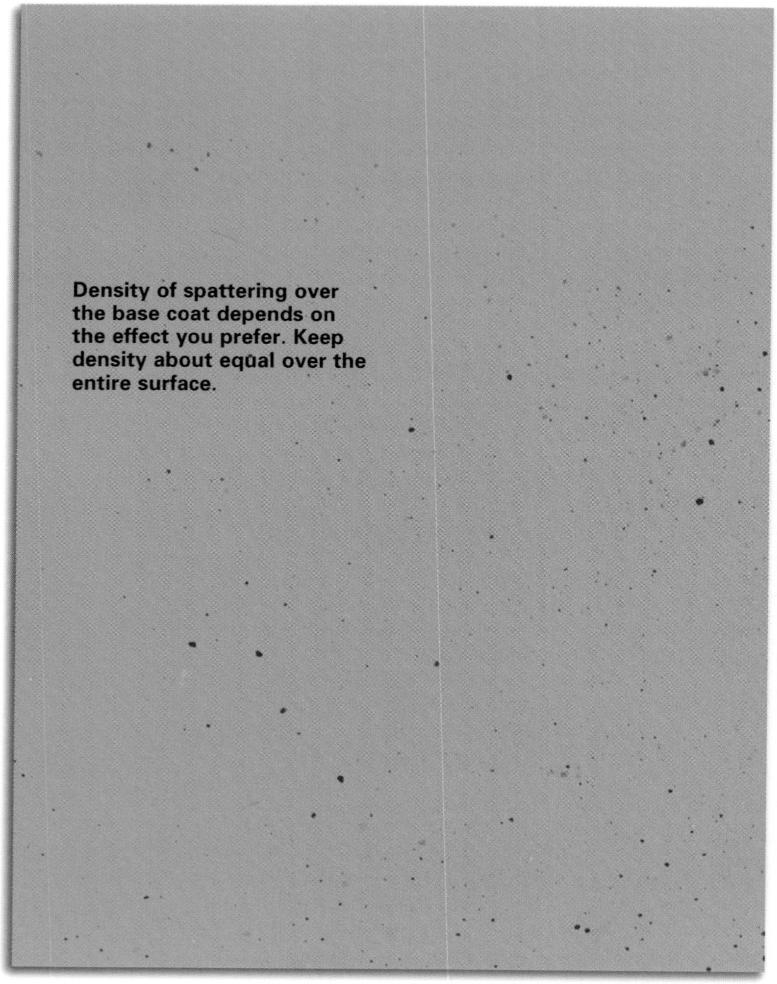

Density of spattering over the base coat depends on the effect you prefer. Keep density about equal over the entire surface.

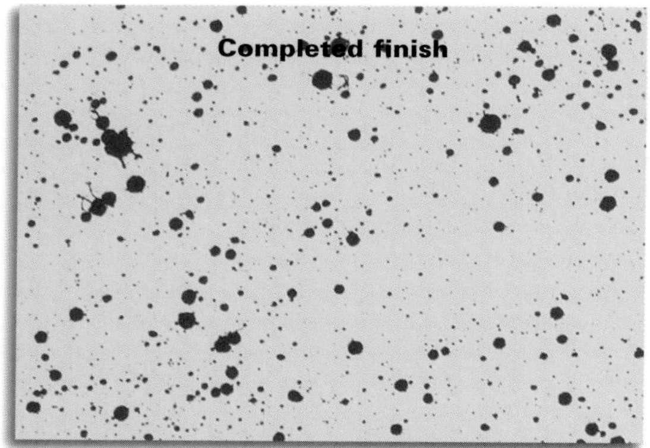

A large, stiff-bristle brush makes large specks.

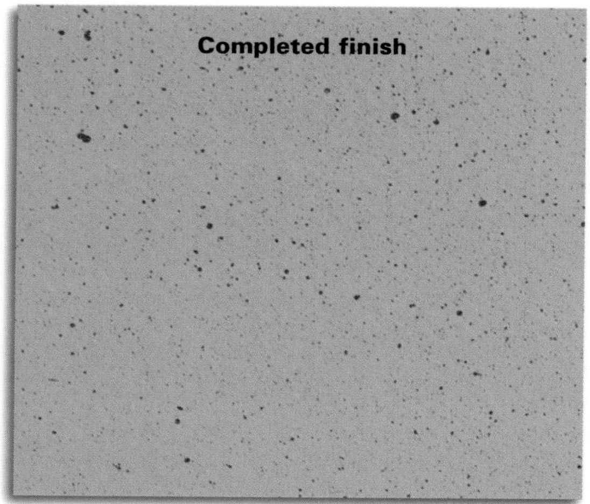

A toothbrush or spatter tool makes small specks. Dark and light colors have been spattered on this sample.

PAINTED LINES

You can paint lines to accent contours or for decoration with liner brushes or a striping tool.

LINER BRUSHES

There are two types of round liner brushes—regular and script liners. Regular liners are used to paint fine lines and tiny dots. Script liners, also known as scroller brushes, have bristles twice as long as a regular liner. They hold more paint than regular liners, but are harder to control.

Liners vary in diameter; sizes range from the small #18/0 to #6. Buy a liner that has good spring and flare, and a fine, even point with no stray hairs.

You also can paint straight, uniform lines by laying out the line with edge tape—like masking tape—and painting with a brush.

PROCEDURE: To paint with a liner, thin the paint to the consistency of ink. Then pull the full length of the bristles through the paint on a palette. Load the paint up to the metal ferrule, then press the brush down so the bristles fan out. Next, lift the brush and turn it over to fill the other side with paint. As you pull the brush out of the paint, twist the handle to make a sharp point on the bristles. If you can't see the fine tip, you've overloaded the brush. If you can't see color on the entire length of the bristles, you've haven't loaded the brush enough.

When you paint with a liner brush, move your entire arm. Let your little finger touch the surface for balance. Trace the line with your little finger; the brush will glide along the surface, following your hand (see right).

Paint fine line work with the tip of the bristles. Paint slowly to allow the paint to move down the bristles. You can change the thickness of your lines by applying more or less pressure to the tip.

You can paint almost any style of lettering with a liner. Apply steady pressure to create letters with even lines or vary the pressure on your brush for different styles of lettering.

STRIPING TOOL

A striping tool applies paint with a roller. Most tools can paint single or multiple lines in one stroke and have an adjustable arm that allows you to follow an edge or guide. Striping tools are ideal for painting long, straight lines.

PROCEDURE: Follow the manufacturer's instructions to thin the paint and load the tool. Move your arm to guide the tool smoothly and steadily for best results.

SUPPLIES

- Paint
- Liner brushes or striping tool
- Edge tape

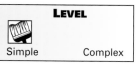

LEVEL

Simple Complex

WORKS WONDERS ON...

You can outline areas or highlight details on any project with painted lines. The lines themselves can be decorative elements too.

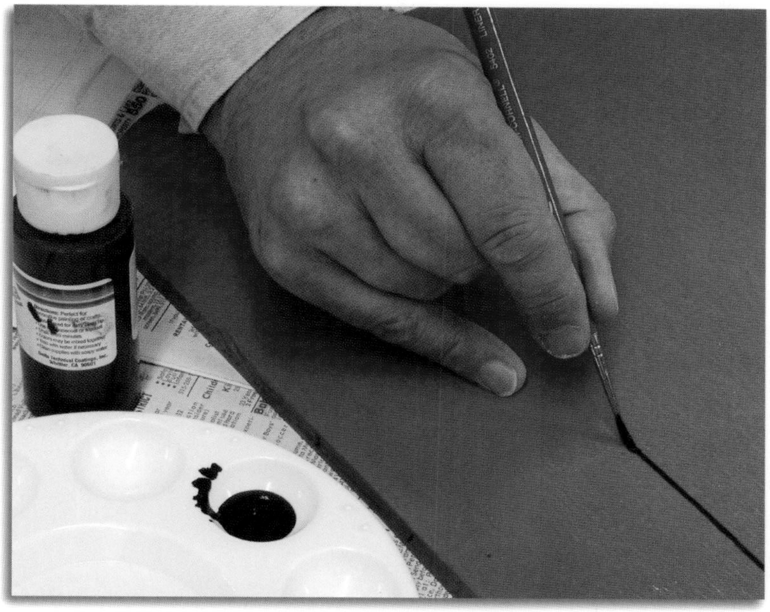

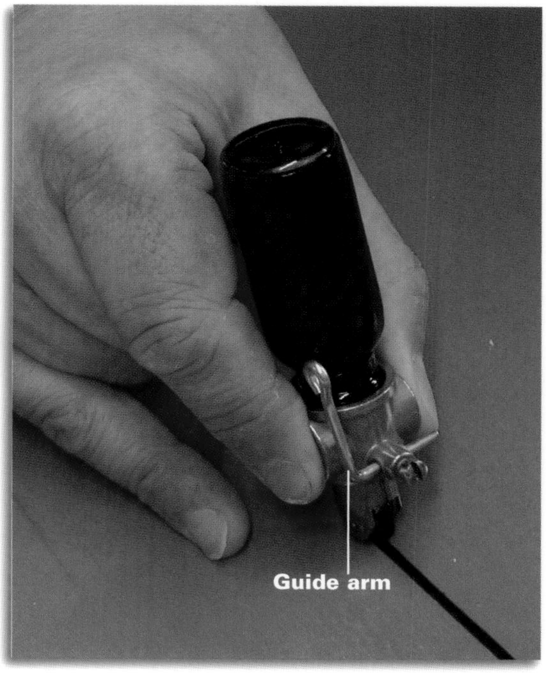

You can paint lines with a liner brush or a striping tool. To use either one, move your arm and let your little finger rest on the work as a guide. The guide arm on the striping tool can be positioned to follow an edge or another guide.

SPONGING

LEVEL

Simple Complex

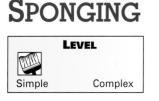

SUPPLIES

- Neutral glazing medium
- Color paint glaze
- Acrylic paint
- Latex wall paint
- Stir stick
- Cellulose sponge, sea sponge, sponging mitt, or sea sponging mitt

Sponging color glaze over paint is most often done to create a random mottled appearance. The combinations of the base coat and the sponging color are unlimited. You can sponge several colors onto a surface too. You also can work sponging into sections of a striped wall (see page 86) or a stenciled border (see page 80).

There are two methods for sponging color: sponging off (a negative technique) and sponging on (a positive technique).

To sponge on color, dip the sponge into the glaze and pounce it on the base-coated surface.

To sponge off color, apply the glaze over the base-coated surface and pounce the clean, damp sponge onto the wet glaze to lift and remove some of the color.

Test different types of sponges to see which look you prefer. Cellulose household sponges leave different impressions and patterns than natural sea sponges.

PROCEDURE:: Prepare and base-coat the surface. Allow the paint to dry.

Mix the glaze for sponging by combining neutral glazing medium with paint or a paint glaze. Always use oil paint with oil-base glaze and acrylic or latex paint with water-base glaze. Refer to the manufacturer's instructions for suggested mixing proportions.

Pour some glaze onto a palette or tray for sponging on; spread it over the base-coated surface for sponging off. For sponging off, glaze only as much of the surface as you can work before the glaze dries.

Dampen the sponge to soften it, then squeeze out the excess moisture. For acrylic or latex paint, dampen the sponge with water; for oil paint, use turpentine. Clean glaze buildup from the sponge periodically for a consistent texture.

WORKS WONDERS ON...

Sponging is a good paint treatment for walls and furniture. Depending on the colors chosen and the sponge texture, the effect can be subtle or bold.

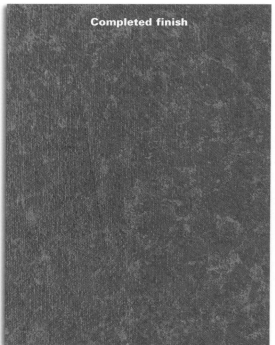

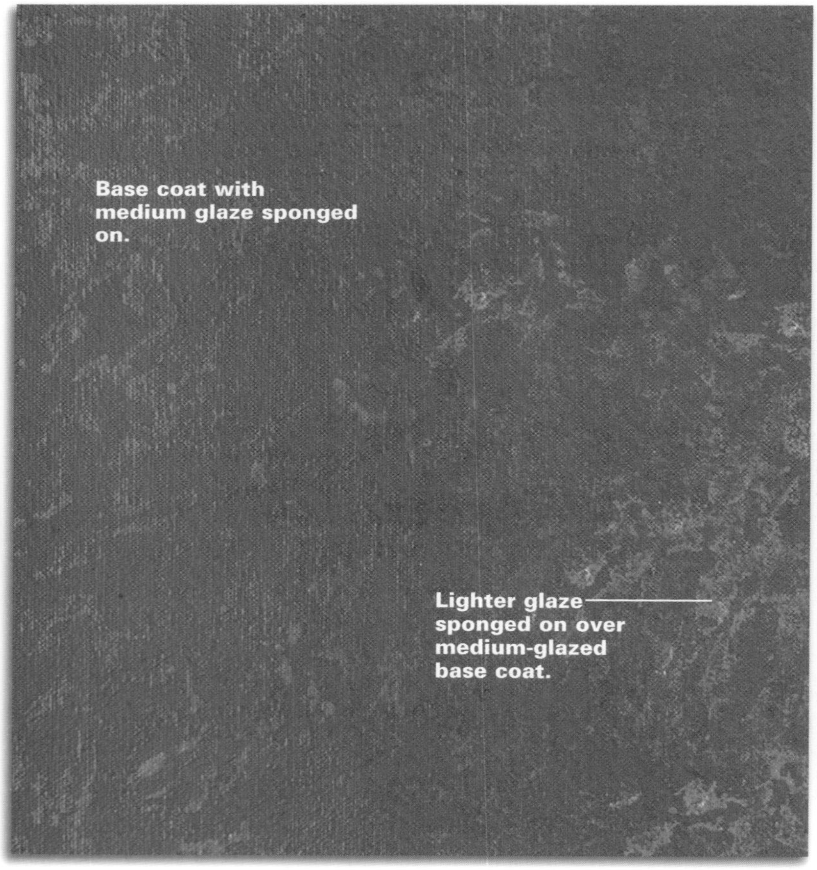
Base coat with medium glaze sponged on.
Lighter glaze sponged on over medium-glazed base coat.

Completed finish

Sponging on, two colors over a dark base coat, using sea sponge. The medium color is sponged on before the lighter one.

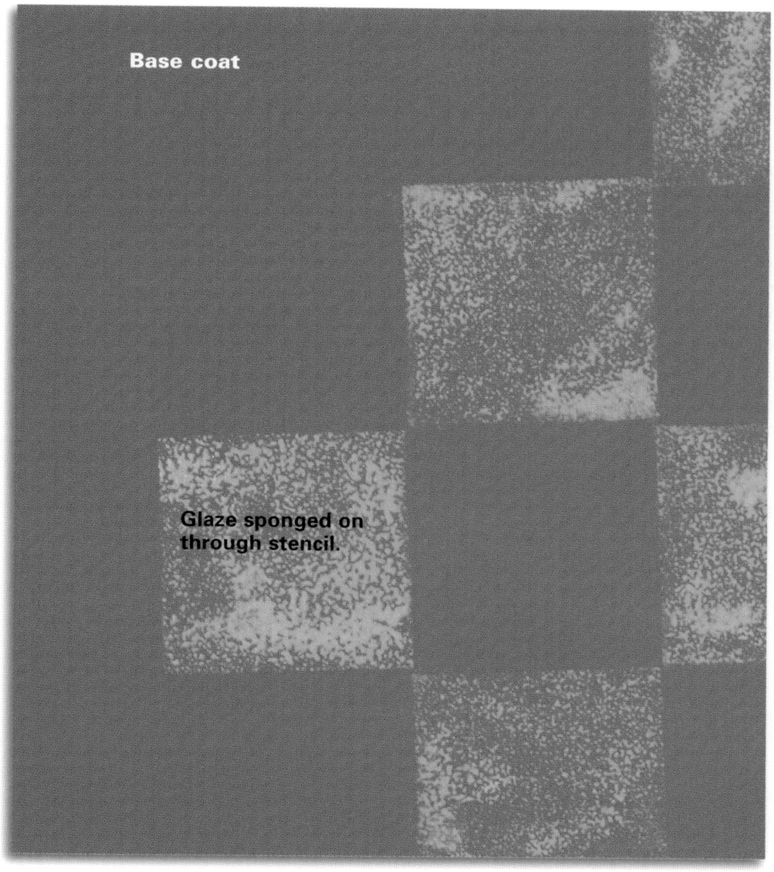
Base coat
Glaze sponged on through stencil.

Paint a checkerboard pattern with a sea sponge and a checkerboard stencil. Hold the stencil against the surface, then stamp the loaded sponge over it.

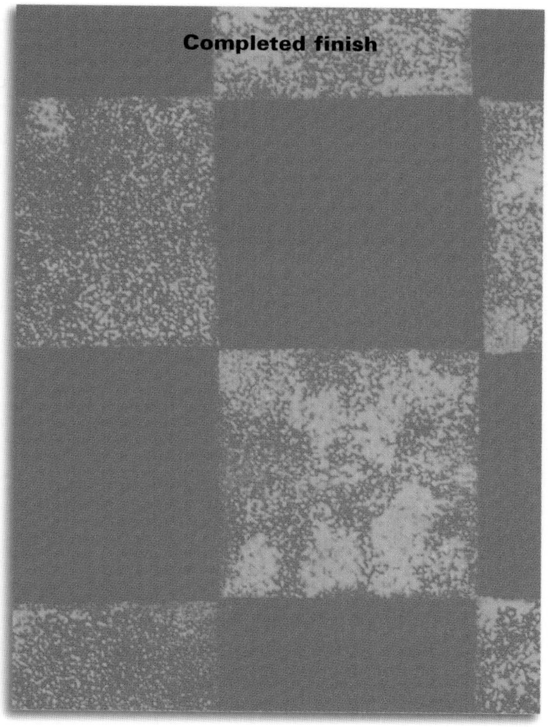
Completed finish

Completed finish

Sponging on several colors, drifting diagonal pattern, using a cellulose sponge.

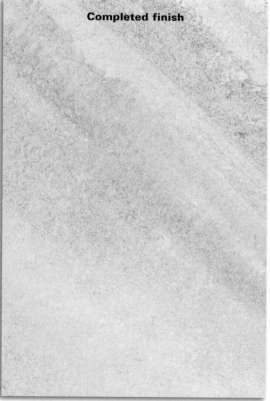

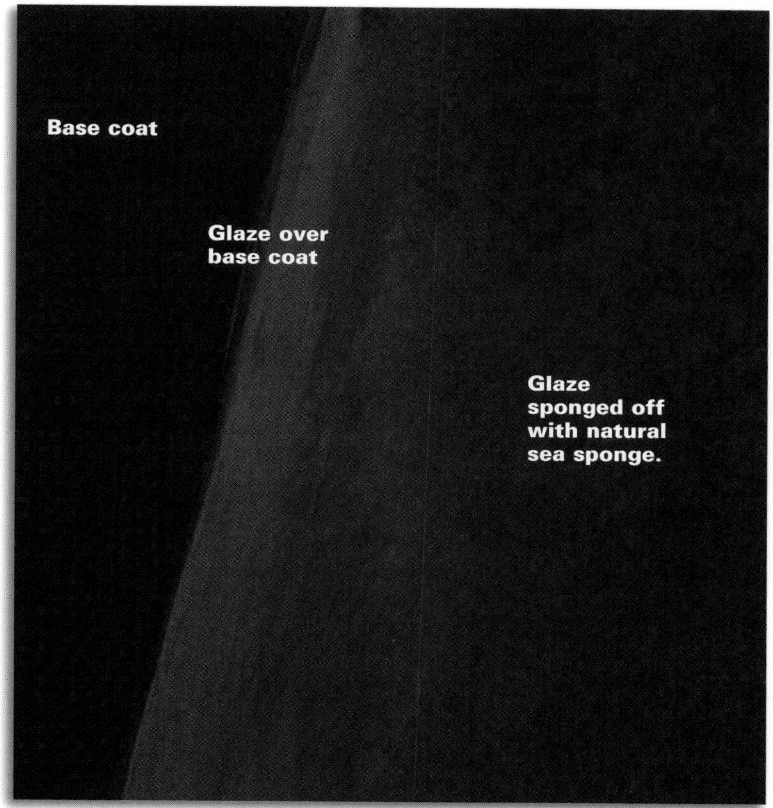
Base coat
Glaze over base coat
Glaze sponged off with natural sea sponge.

Sponging off, medium glaze over a dark base coat.

STENCILING

LEVEL

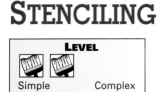

Simple Complex

SUPPLIES

- Paint
- Low-tack masking tape
- Crafts knife
- Precut stencils or acetate stencil material
- Stencil brush
- Glass or suitable cutting surface

For centuries, decorators have painted repeating patterns on walls and furniture by using simple stencils, paint, and brushes. Acetate stencil material is easier to use than the old paper or cardboard stencils, which required special care to keep the paint from seeping under them.

You can buy precut stencils at crafts stores or cut your own from stencil acetate, also available at crafts stores. The best stencil material is glossy on one side and frosted on the other—paint is less likely to stick to the glossy side, and the frosted side resists sliding around on the surface. Cut stencils with a heated stencil-cutting tool or a crafts knife.

PROCEDURE:: Tape your stencil to the base-coated surface with repositionable tape or low-tack masking tape. You can adhere it with nonpermanent spray-on adhesive too.

Unthinned acrylic paint, heavy-bodied stencil paint, or stencil paint crayons are the best choices for stenciling. Paint that's too thin will seep under the stencil edge and make a mess.

Load the stencil brush by tapping the end into paint spread on a tray or palette. Load it with only a little paint; wipe off any excess onto a paper towel. Hold the brush perpendicular to the surface. With a light circular motion or a pouncing motion (whichever one you prefer), paint from the edge of the stencil to the center. Use a light touch so paint won't seep under the stencil.

To create contrast in the design, let the base color show in the center. You can achieve different effects by painting the stencil with a sponge, a rag, or even spray paint. Experiment with different paint applications to find the most pleasing effect for your project.

WORKS WONDERS ON...

Stenciling is an ideal way to paint borders on walls, either at the ceiling or along a chair rail. Whole walls can be stenciled too. Ornamental designs are often stenciled on furniture and cabinetry.

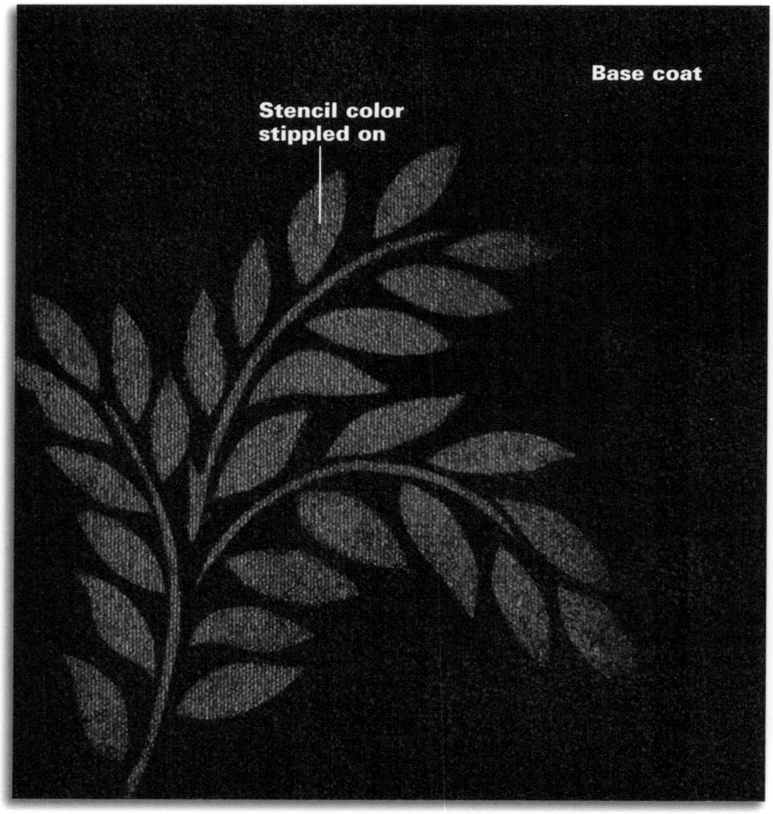

A light color stenciled onto a dark base coat with a stippling brush.

STENCILING OVER ANTIQUING

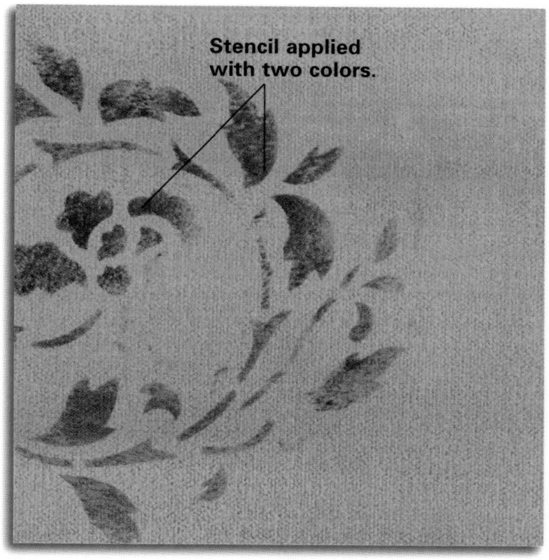

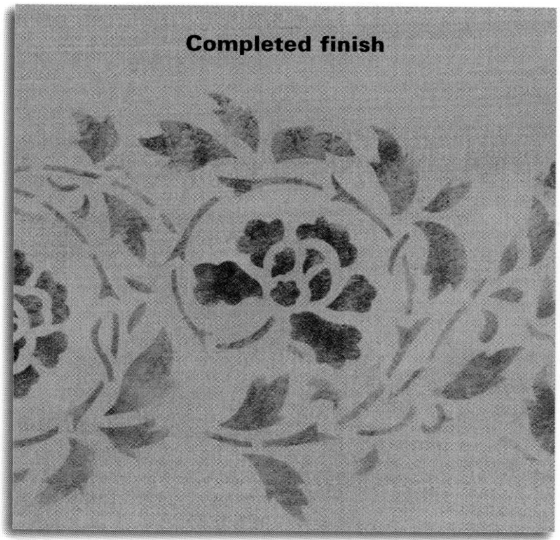

This two-color stenciling has been applied over an antiqued surface. Stenciling over another finish lets the design stand out more.

ANTIQUING OVER STENCILING

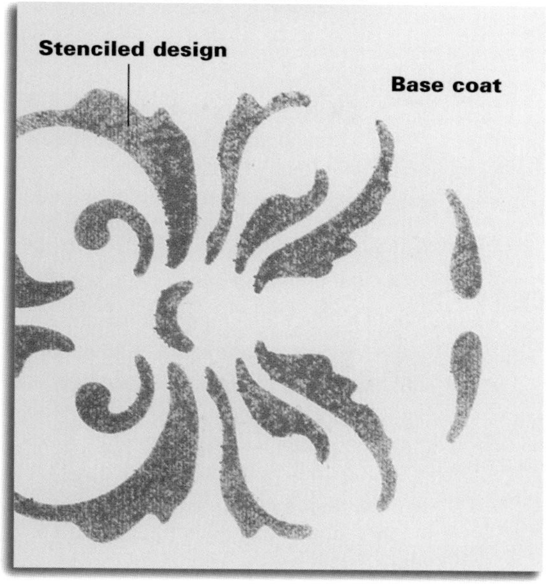

You can stencil a surface, then apply antiquing glaze over it, as shown left and below.

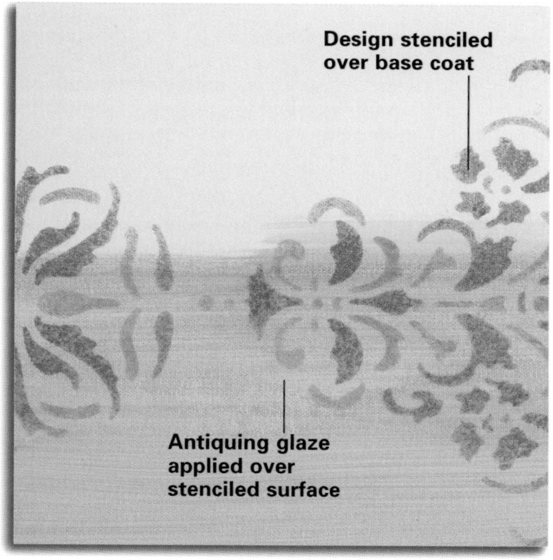

Glaze applied over the stencil below and below left has been woodgrained.

WOOD GRAINING OVER STENCILING

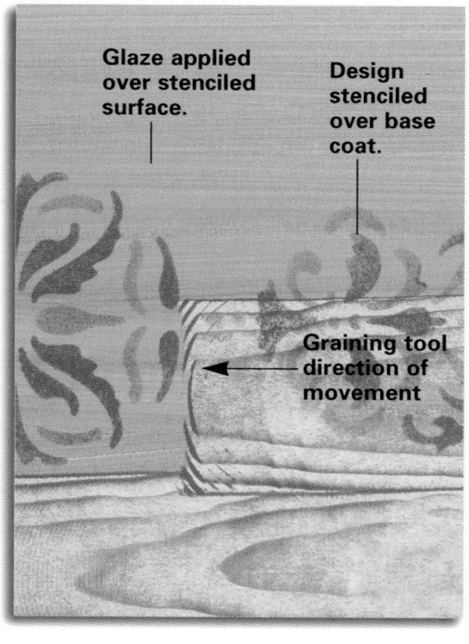

STIPPLING

LEVEL

Simple Complex

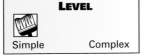

SUPPLIES

- Stippling brushes or stippling pad with rubber bristles
- Glaze
- Pliable paintbrush
- Acrylic paint or decorator glaze for tinting
- Damp cloth

Stippling is a way to blend colors and add subtle texture to a glazed surface. The resulting effect can mimic any look, from floor tile to the sky and clouds. Stippling can be done as a positive or negative technique, using a brush or stippling pad.

POSITIVE TECHNIQUE

Glaze is stippled onto the base-coated surface in the positive application. Start by base-coating the surface. Let the base coat dry.

Mix neutral glaze with tinted glaze or acrylic paint to make the stippling color you want.

Dip the stippling brush bristles into the glaze. Pounce the brush a few times on a clean disposable plate to work the glaze into the bristles. Then, pounce the glaze onto the surface. Work one area at a time, taking care to keep the stippling pattern and texture uniform. Reload the brush as needed. Periodically wipe the brush on a damp cloth to keep glaze from building up in the bristles.

NEGATIVE TECHNIQUE

In the negative technique, glaze is applied to the surface, then removed with the stippling brush or tool. Base-coat the surface. After it dries, roll or brush the glaze onto a small section of the surface. Apply the glaze to only as much surface as you can stipple before the glaze dries.

While the glaze is still wet, pounce the surface with the brush bristles to remove some of the glaze. Leave a narrow wet edge of glaze as you get near the end of each section so you can apply glaze to the adjoining section and continue stippling without creating a distinct line. Wipe the brush bristles on a damp cloth or rag to remove glaze buildup.

WORKS WONDERS ON...

Stippling is suited to most surfaces—walls, woodwork, furniture, and small items. The technique can suggest many textures, from leather to stone, depending on the colors selected and the degree of stippling.

Glaze coat applied over base coat then worked with stippler.
Base coat

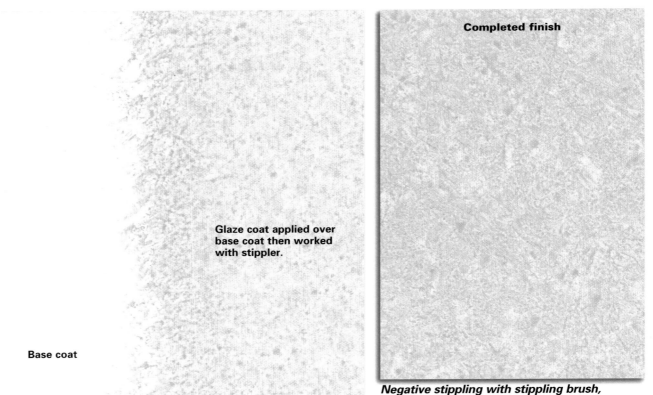

Completed finish

Negative stippling with stippling brush, medium glaze over a light base coat.

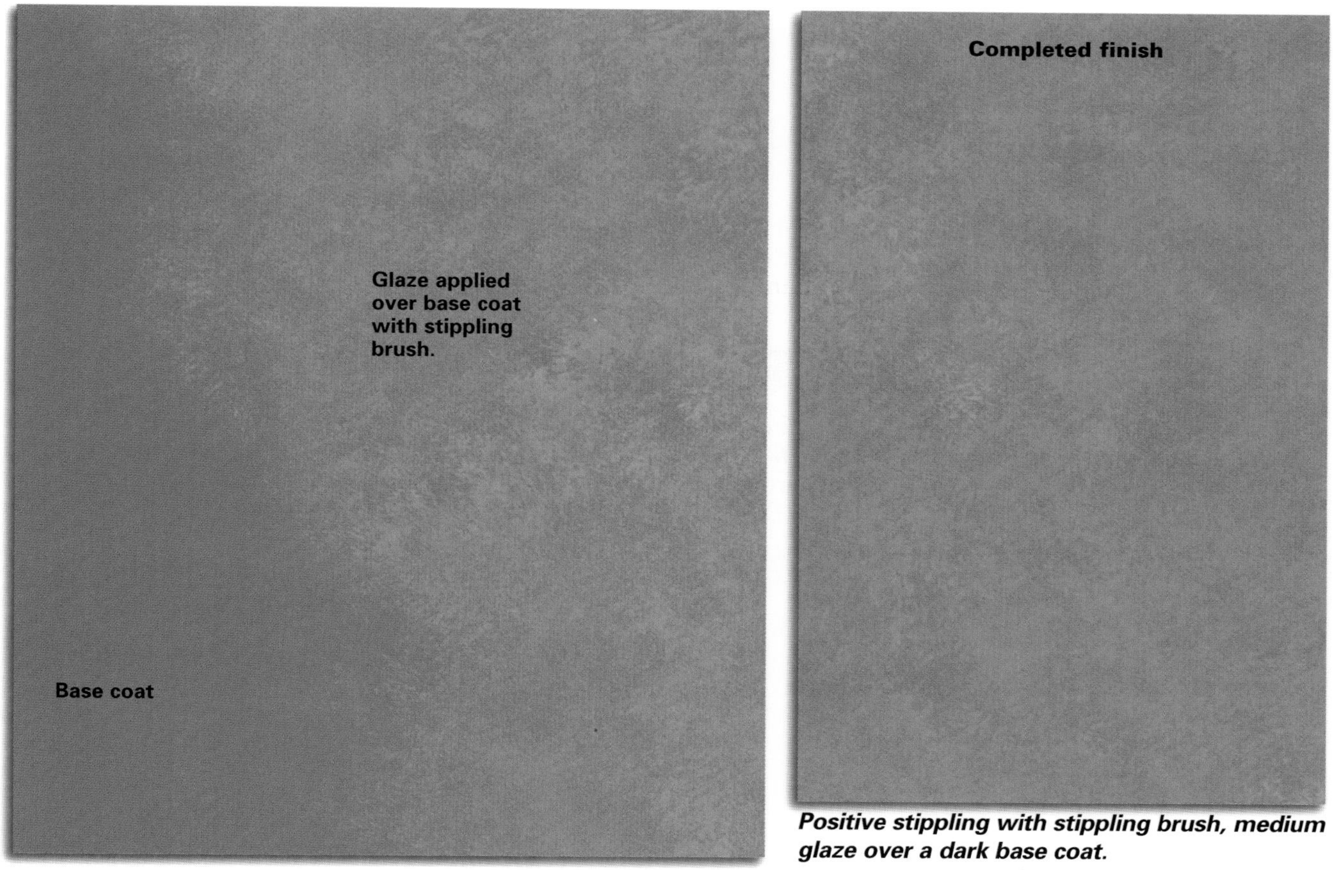

Positive stippling with stippling brush, medium glaze over a dark base coat.

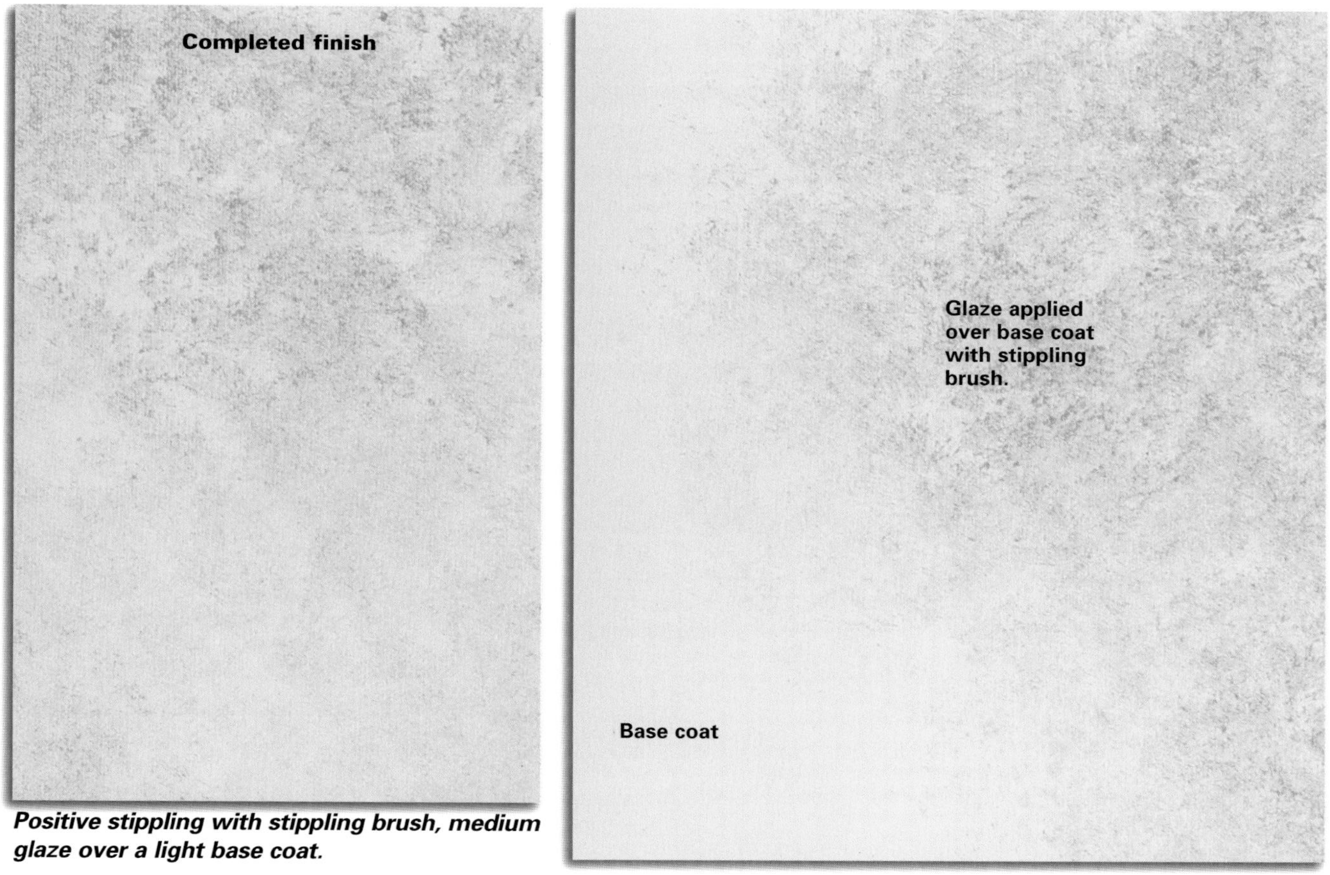

Positive stippling with stippling brush, medium glaze over a light base coat.

STONE BLOCKS AND BRICKS

LEVEL
Simple — Complex

SUPPLIES

- Wall paint
- Glaze
- Stippling brushes or stippling pad with rubber bristles
- Rectangular cellulose sponge
- Foam brush
- Paint trays or plates
- Masking tape

After masking mortar lines with tape, apply the glazes for the stone finish with a stippling brush.

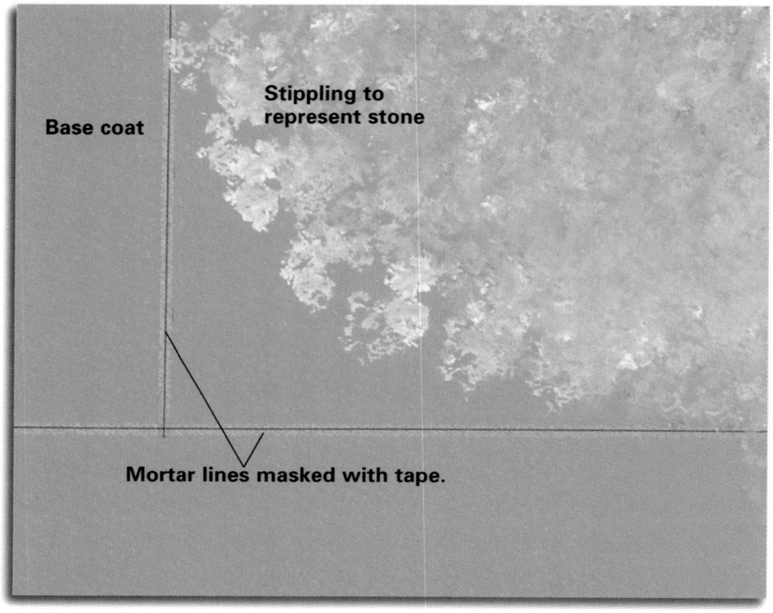

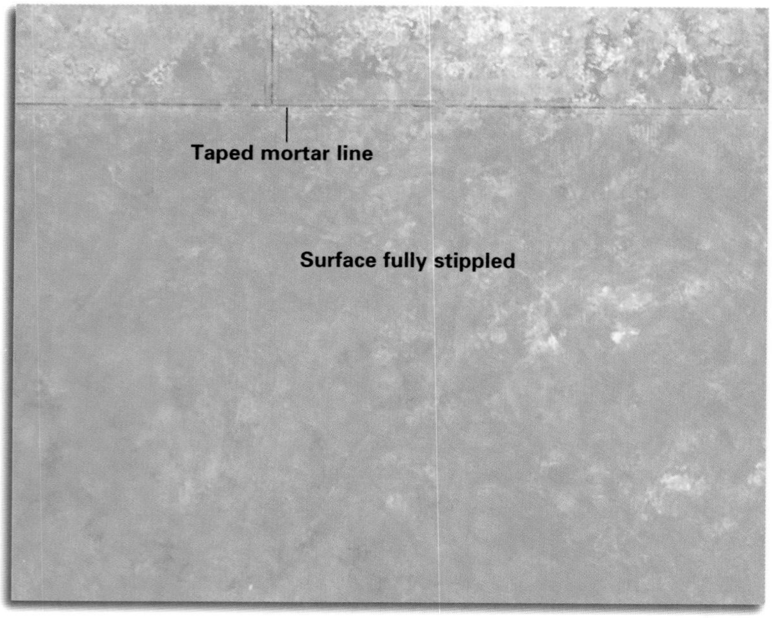

Stone blocks and bricks usually have uniform vertical and horizontal mortar joints between them. In the painting techniques for these finishes, the gray base coat is exposed to represent the mortar lines.

STONE BLOCKS

Base-coat the surface with gray wall paint in a flat or satin sheen. Allow the paint to dry thoroughly.

Mix the glaze colors (beige and tan were used for our example). You can use either water-base or oil-base glaze and colors. A 50-50 mix of color and neutral glaze works well. You can make a mix with more neutral glaze than paint to achieve a lighter glaze effect.

Lay out the block forms on the wall, using a level, plumb bob, and pencil. Draw the block shapes on the surface, starting from a bottom corner and working up and across. Stagger the joints. Make the blocks about 8 inches tall and about 16 inches long. You can make them other sizes to match the scale of the surface or make blocks of varied sizes.

Place tape along the layout lines to create the mortar joints. The mortar lines will be the width of the tape you use. (Our example uses ⅛-inch graphic arts tape, available from art supply stores.) Smooth the tape along the joint lines.

Pour some of each glaze color onto disposable plates or paint trays. Put one color on each plate.

Dip the tip of a stippling brush into one of the color glazes. You can apply one color at a time or use two stippling brushes.

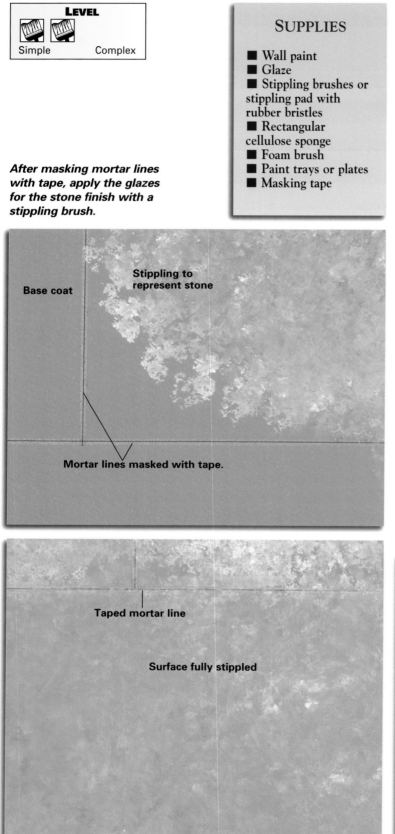

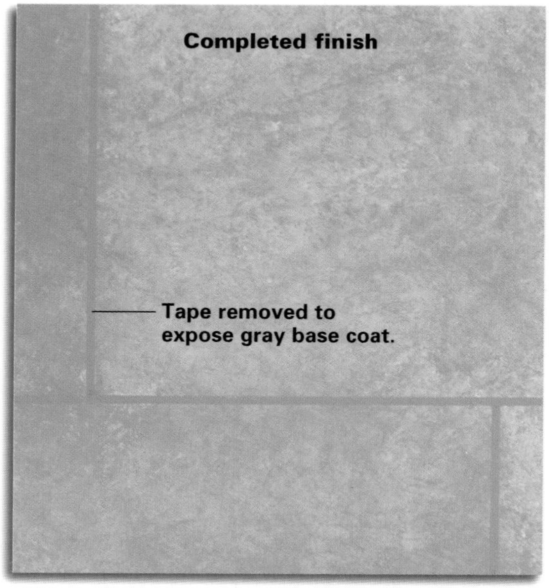

Rapidly pounce the brush onto the surface of one block with one color, then another. Apply the color randomly, and stipple the surface until it looks rough and stony. Don't stipple too much; the more you do, the softer or smoother the paint finish will appear.

Repeat the stippling, one block at a time, until all the blocks are completed.

For realism, the stone blocks should look different from each other. Make some darker in color than others and give some a different texture than others.

Carefully remove the tape from the surface.

BRICK

Brick pattern designs can be stamped onto a surface with a cellulose sponge. The bricks in the example were stamped with the green sponge shown on page 29.

Base-coat the surface. The color will show as the mortar-joint color. Our example uses gray for the base coat.

Mix the glaze color. A brick-red glaze is shown, but you can make your bricks any color. For painted, mixed, or distressed bricks, you can use several glaze colors.

Pour each glaze color onto a separate disposable plate or paint tray. Dip the face of the rectangular sponge into the glaze. Or you can stroke random colors onto the face of the sponge with a 1-inch foam brush. When all or some of the paint colors have been laid onto the surface of the sponge, stamp the brick pattern onto the surface.

Space the stamped shapes, leaving a uniform space between them to represent mortar joints. Stagger the vertical joints between the bricks for a realistic look.

You can stamp the brick design more than once if you want to change the color, shape, or texture.

WORKS WONDERS ON...

Stone and brick are good finishes for walls and other surfaces that might be built of masonry. The stone finish without grout lines could give small objects the look of being carved from stone.

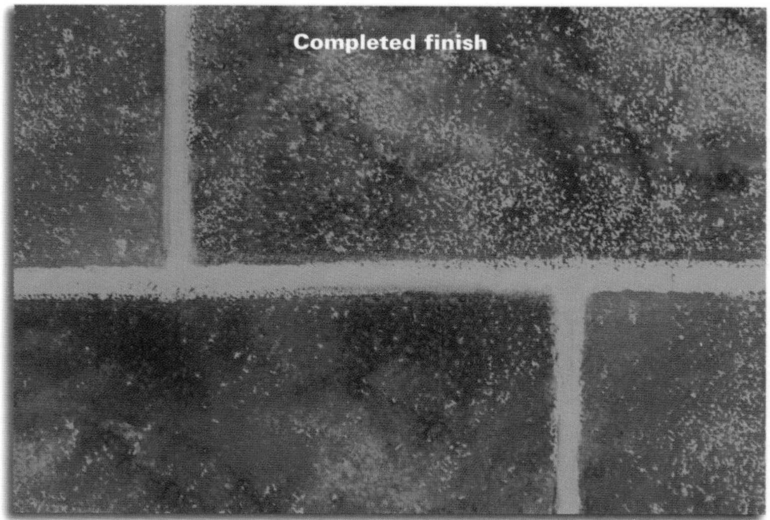
Completed finish

Stagger the mortar lines, represented by the base coat, for a realistic look.

Space stamped bricks to make mortar lines.
Bricks stamped with cellulose sponge.
Base coat

Bricks are stamped with a 3½×7-inch sponge. Spacing between the stamped bricks reveals the gray base coat, which represents mortar joints.

STRIPING

SUPPLIES

- Paint
- Neutral glazing medium
- Ruler and tape measure
- Pencil
- Plumb bob and line
- Low-tack masking tape
- Sea sponge

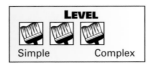

LEVEL

Simple Complex

Stripes emphasize the height of walls and look distinctive in any room. Painting stripes is time-consuming, but it's easy, and the results are well worth the investment of time. You can paint simple stripes of any width—or of multiple widths. You can enhance the stripes by ragging, sponging, or combing glaze over some or all of them. Stripes of clear, gloss varnish applied over flat or satin paint creates a subtle, elegant look. You can paint bright, bold stripes or use calm colors, following any color scheme.

For the best effect, make sure the stripes are plumb, uniform, and centered on the focal point of the wall (see pages 32–33).

Decide whether the stripes will be the same width or varied, then determine the width and spacing of the stripes. Lay out the stripes so they wrap around inside corners, since walls are not always straight.

In the design shown below, 4-inch-wide terra-cotta stripes alternate with 2-inch-wide ivory stripes.

PROCEDURE: Base-coat the wall and let it dry thoroughly. For the terra-cotta and ivory stripes, the base coat is ivory because the terra-cotta color will cover it better than ivory paint would cover the darker color.

At the top of the wall, lay out the stripe pattern with pencil marks. For the example below, you would make a mark 4 inches from your starting point, another mark 2 inches from that one, then 4 inches, and so forth.

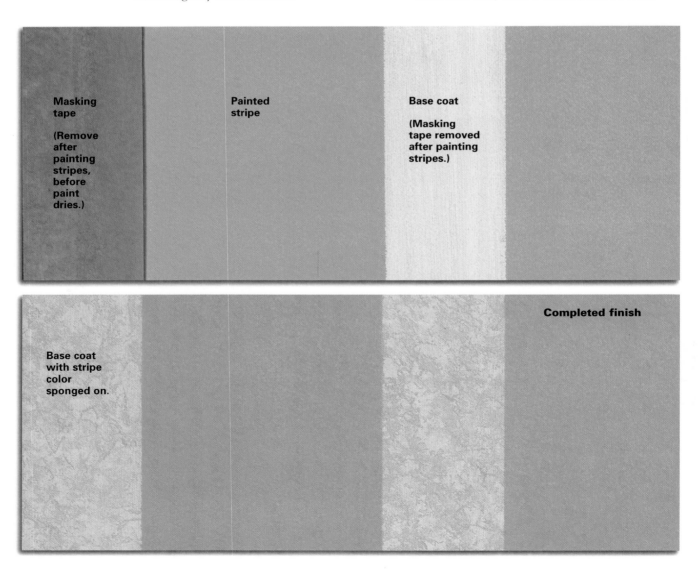

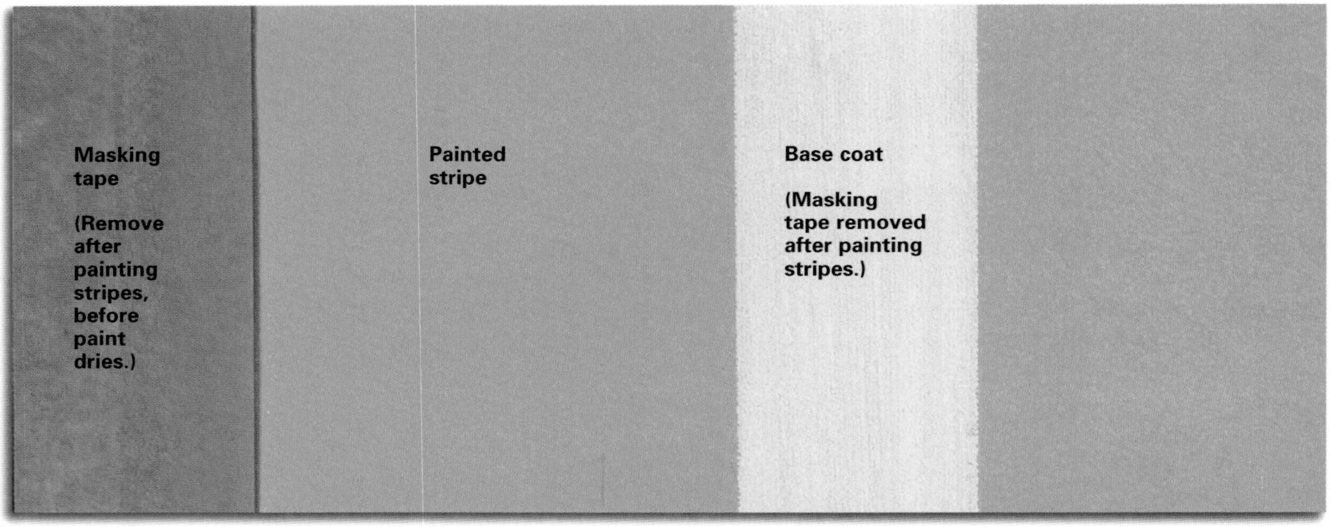

Use a plumb line to mark each vertical stripe edge. Mask off the 4-inch stripes. Seal down the edges of the masking tape firmly to prevent paint from wicking under it. Then paint the terra-cotta stripes with a roller. (You could use such techniques as sponging, ragging, or stippling for the stripes.) Remove the masking tape before the paint dries to prevent a ragged edge.

To add more texture, mask the ivory stripes and antique them with a mixture of the terra-cotta paint and glazing medium. (Let the terra-cotta stripes dry before you put masking tape on them.) Sponge or rag the antiquing in a vertical pattern. Remove the tape before the paint dries.

For an overall softening of the stripes, sponge a glaze mixture over all the stripes. Choose a color slightly darker than the darkest stripe. Let the paint dry thoroughly.

WORKS WONDERS ON...

Striping is primarily a wall treatment. It could be effective on some furniture, such as room divider screens, or on inset panels. Keep the width of the stripes in scale with the size of the surface.

ADDED TOUCHES

Mix the second color with glazing medium for a more translucent effect that will help the stripes complement each other more dramatically.

Add a pinstripe in a contrasting color or metallic gold. To do this, run 1/4-inch-wide tape (the type used for automotive pinstriping) vertically along the inside edges of the wider stripe. Next, run a strip of 1-inch-wide masking tape along each side of the 1/4-inch tape. Peel away the 1/4-inch tape and dab color into the exposed area to create your stripe. Remove the masking tape quickly.

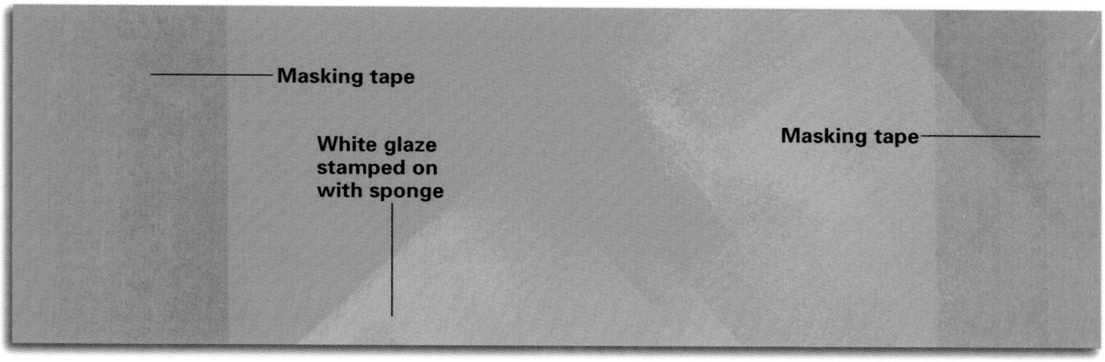

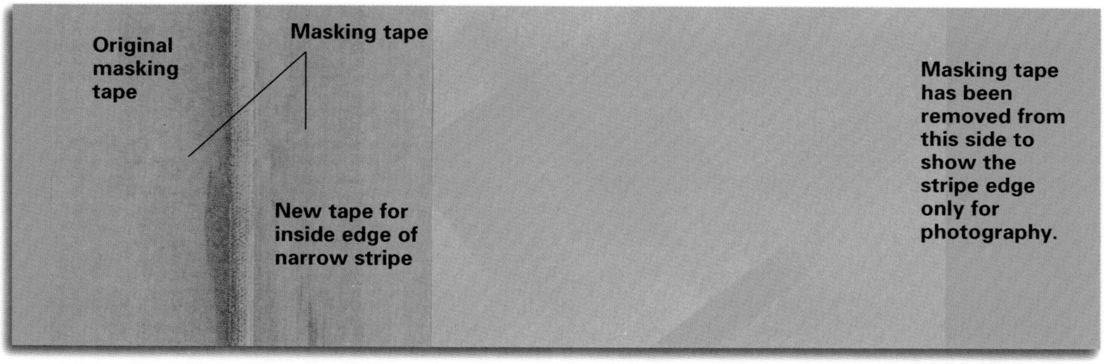

The wide, outlined stripe in the bottom photo is painted with several techniques. White glaze is sponge-stamped onto the base coat (top photo) for the wide stripe. The narrow stripes are masked off and a glaze darker than the base color is applied (middle photo). The white and dark lines are hand-painted (see page 77).

TORTOISESHELL

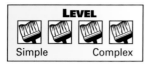

LEVEL
Simple — Complex

SUPPLIES

- Gold-color paint
- Copper-color glaze
- Burnt sienna glaze
- Burnt umber glaze
- Clear glaze
- Round brush
- Badger brush or mop
- Toothbrush
- Turpentine

The mottled coloration of tortoiseshell can be imitated by painting a series of burnt umber, burnt sienna, and copper dots over a gold base, then blending them together. Apply the paint spots over a wet glaze coat (called wet-on-wet technique) to promote better blending.

PROCEDURE: Apply a sealer to the workpiece, then paint it with a base coat of metallic gold paint. Apply several coats if needed for a smooth surface. Let the paint dry.

Apply a coat of clear glaze to the surface with a sponge brush. You will paint onto the wet glaze, so cover only as much area as you can finish before the glaze dries. If the glaze appears to be drying while you work, lightly mist the surface with water to rewet it.

Using a round brush, dab on circular spots of copper-color glaze about ½ inch in diameter. Don't worry about making them exactly round. Vary the size of the dots, and space them several dots apart, allowing the gold color to show through. Work quickly while the surface is wet, and apply the spots of paint in a diagonal pattern.

Next, mix small dollops of burnt sienna and burnt umber with enough clear neutral glaze to achieve a creamy consistency. Dab on spots of the burnt sienna glaze, about the same size as the copper-color spots, but closer together. Add burnt umber spots. Allow each color to show, but overlap them as shown in the photos on the opposite page. Add dabs of the gold base-coat color on top.

Use a soft mop brush or badger brush to pounce and mop over the surface, following the same diagonal. This will pull and blur the colors together. The clear glaze on the surface helps blend and blur the colors. Do not blend too much—keep some distinction among the colors.

For additional texture, pockmark the finish by spattering the wet surface with turpentine, using an old toothbrush. Spatter thinned burnt umber, then thinned burnt sienna over the surface. Let the finish dry thoroughly, then protect it with a clear glaze top coat.

WORKS WONDERS ON...

The shells of some turtles were once used to make combs, furniture inlays, and other decorative items. This painted finish mimics that look. It works best as an accent on furniture or small items.

Apply spots of burnt umber, burnt sienna, and copper-color glaze over the gold-color base coat randomly in a diagonal pattern. Allow the base color to show through in places.

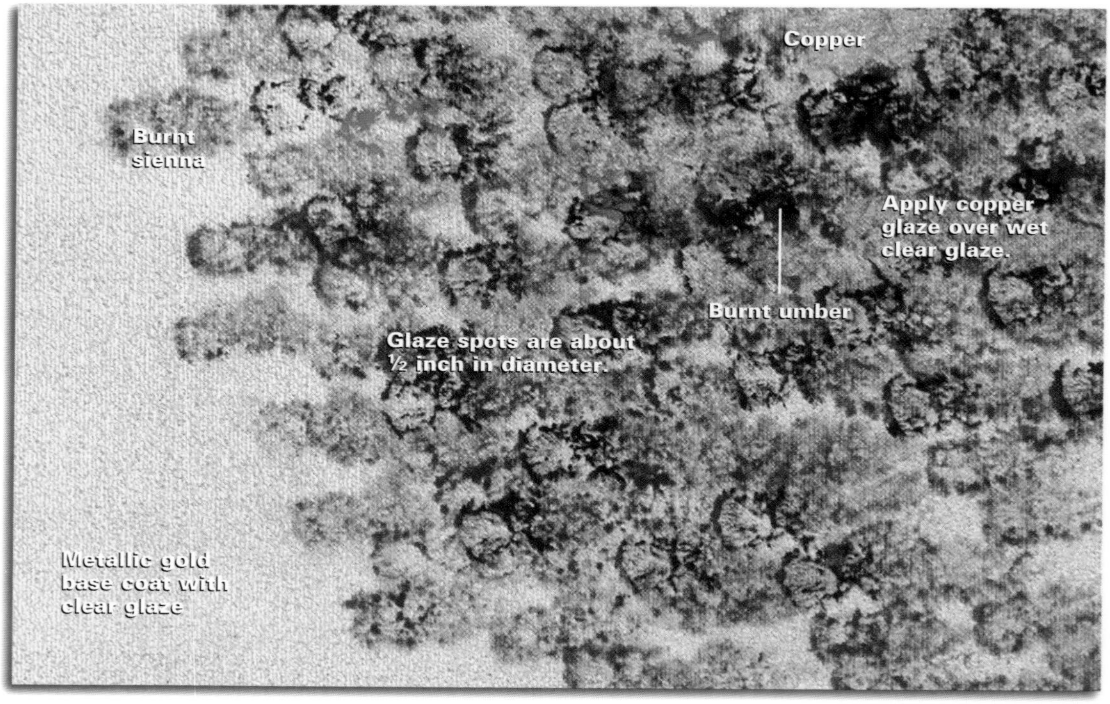
Copper
Burnt sienna
Apply copper glaze over wet clear glaze.
Burnt umber
Glaze spots are about ½ inch in diameter.
Metallic gold base coat with clear glaze

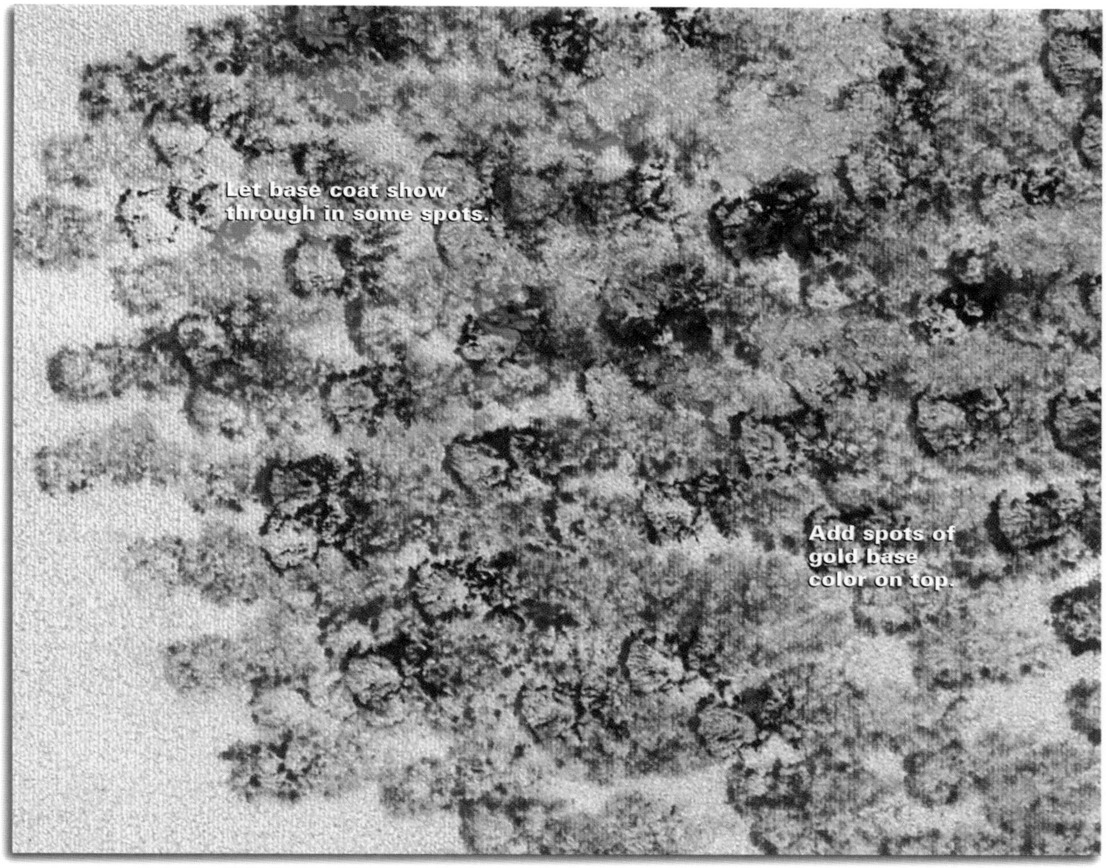
Let base coat show through in some spots.
Add spots of gold base color on top.

The color spots are distinct before blending. Spots of the gold base color have been added on top of the wet glazes to blend in.

After blending with a badger brush, the colors are less distinct but still recognizable. Avoid blending the spots into a uniform color.

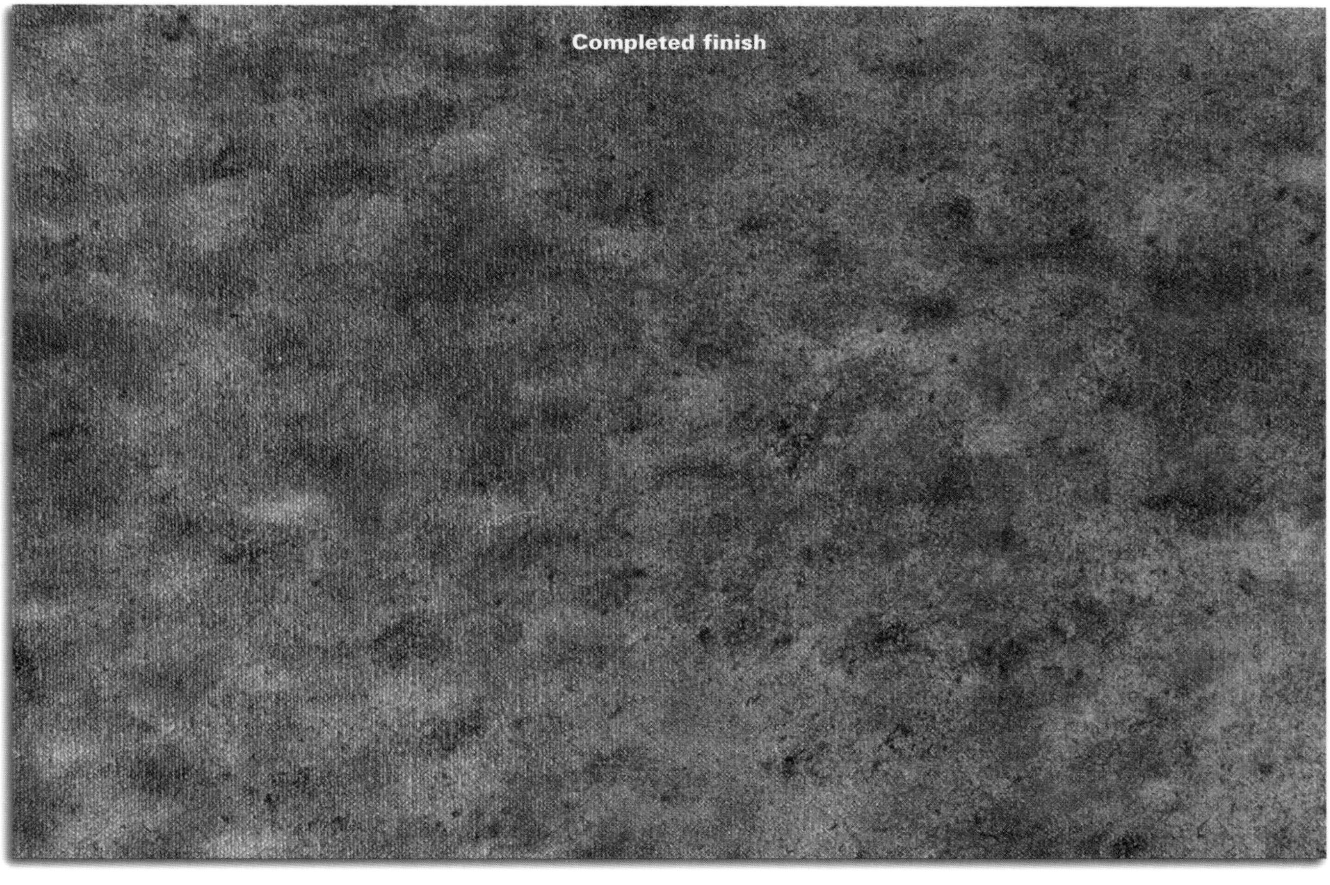
Completed finish

WEATHERED METALS

LEVEL

Simple Complex

VERDIGRIS SUPPLIES

- Copper or bronze paint
- Turquoise acrylic paint
- Water-base neutral glaze
- Verdigris tool
- Spray bottle

Attach the soft loop side of hook-and-loop fastener material to a putty knife to make the verdigris tool.

Paint techniques can imitate weathered, aged metals, even on nonmetal items. For small items, visit a hobby shop that serves model builders and model railroaders. Most of these stores carry assorted spray-on and brush-on paints that provide amazingly realistic representations of rusty, dirty, worn, and sun-faded paint. Refer to the manufacturer's instructions when using these products.

Here are two techniques suited to surfaces of all sizes—verdigris and oxidized iron.

Copper and bronze take on a rich, greenish patina with time and oxidation. Kits are available that create the patina chemically through application of a corrosive solution to copper or bronze paint that has a high metallic content (or to the metals themselves). Crafts stores and many home centers sell the kits.

Here is a method for achieving the look of patinated copper or bronze with paint.

PROCEDURE: Prepare the surface, then apply one or two coats of copper- (shown) or bronze-color paint for the base coat. The base coat needs to look old and weathered itself, so use flat or semigloss paint rather than glossy. Allow the base coat to dry.

Make the verdigris tool, shown in the photograph above, from a 2-inch plastic putty knife and the soft side of hook-and-loop fastener material. Cut a piece of the fastener material large enough to wrap around the end of the putty knife. Tape the material to the blade end, allowing it to overhang the end of the scraper. Cut vertical slits into the material, creating a brush.

Make the turquoise glaze by mixing acrylic crafts paint and water-base neutral glaze. Mix the paint and glaze in roughly equal portions.

Mist the surface with water, using a plant mister or a spray bottle, such as an empty window cleaner bottle.

Then, dip the tip of the verdigris tool into the turquoise glaze. Pat, smear, and rub the glaze randomly over the surface, but don't cover the surface entirely.

If the color gets too intense, spray the surface with water. If the glaze runs slightly, work the brush into it to make a worn, weathered look. The aged verdigris finish should look nonuniform, as if it was the result of action by rain, wind, and sun. A faded, splotchy effect is just what you want.

WORKS WONDERS ON...

Verdigris, oxidized iron, and other metal finishes work well as an accent or as a prime finish on small items. They are good for planters, vases, urns, and weather vane ornaments that are used inside but could once have been outside.

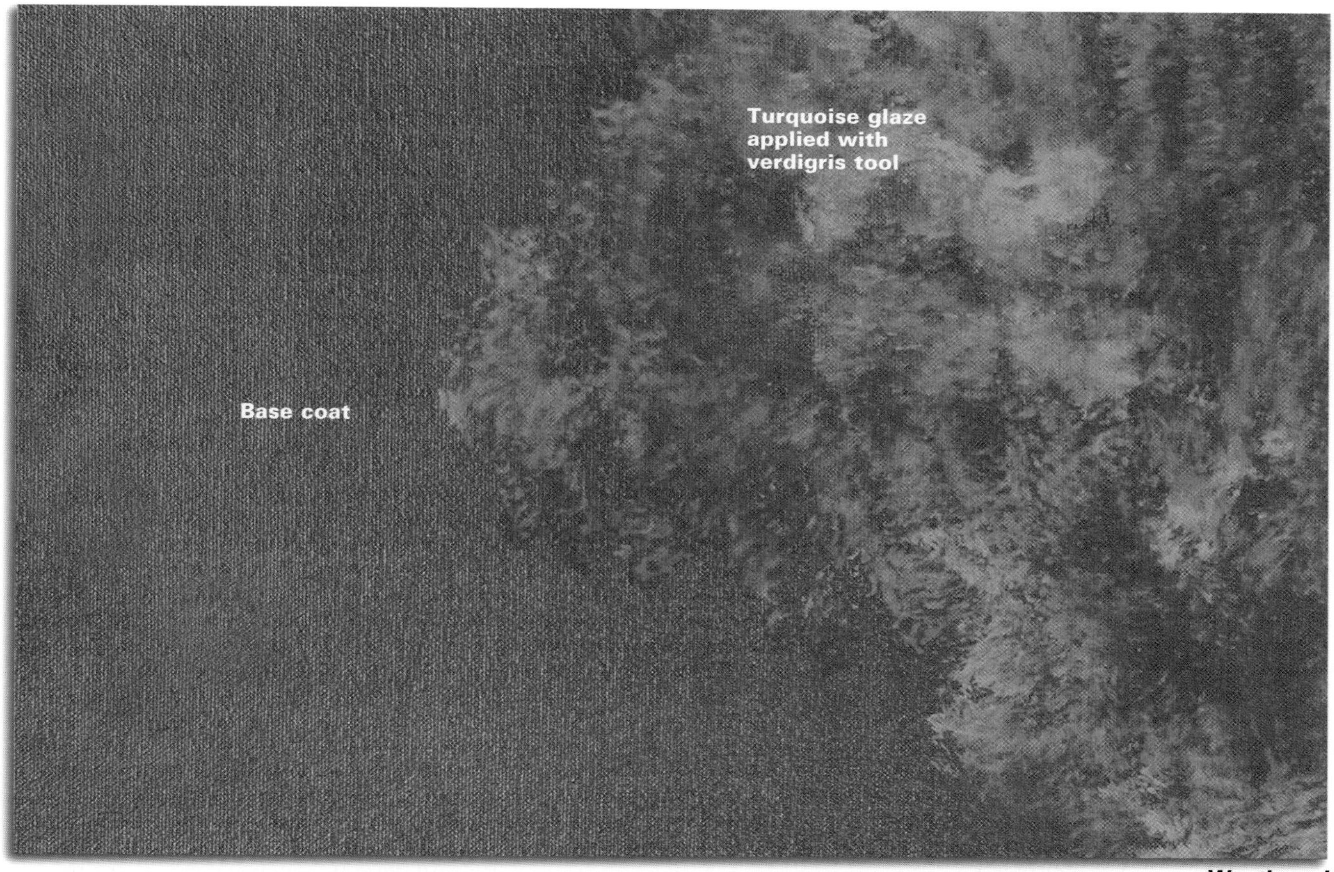

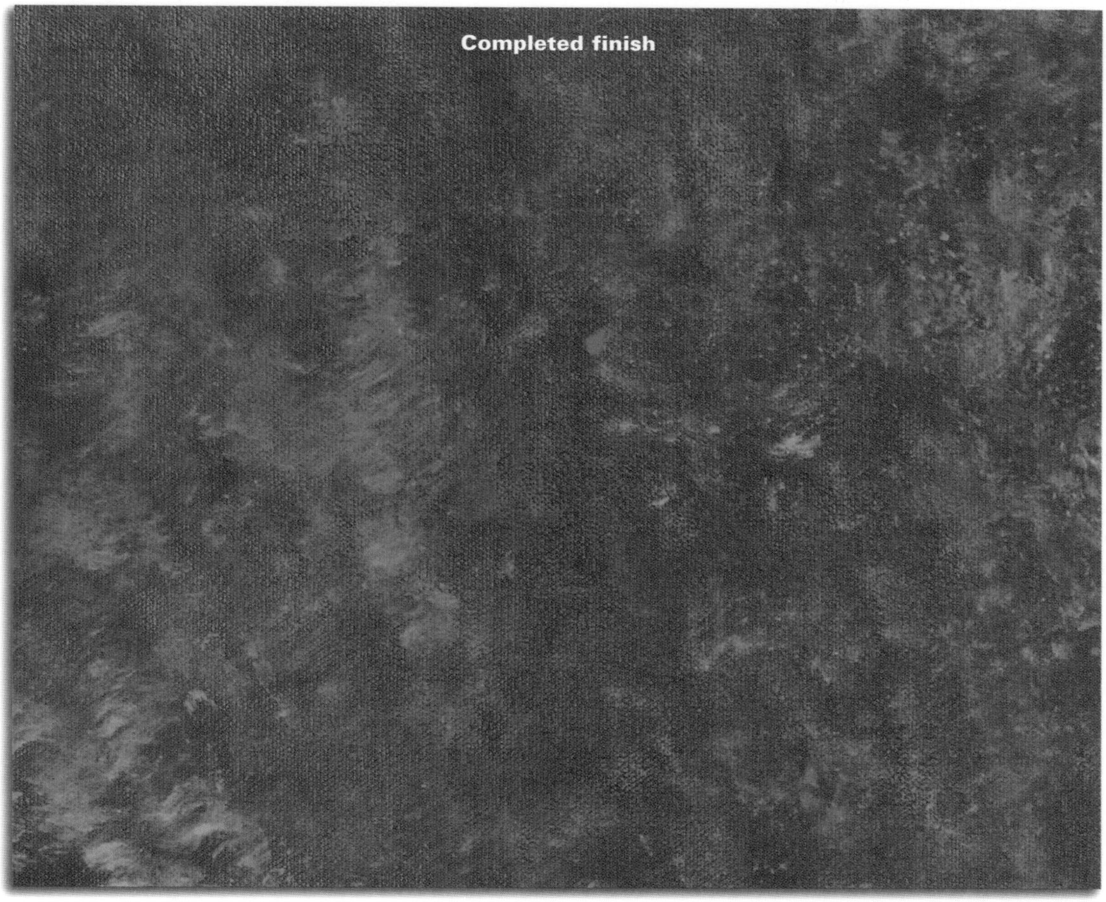

Weathered copper takes on a green patina.

Allow some of the copper-color base coat to show through the glazed areas. Vary the size and density of the areas for realism.

WEATHERED METALS
continued

LEVEL
Simple Complex

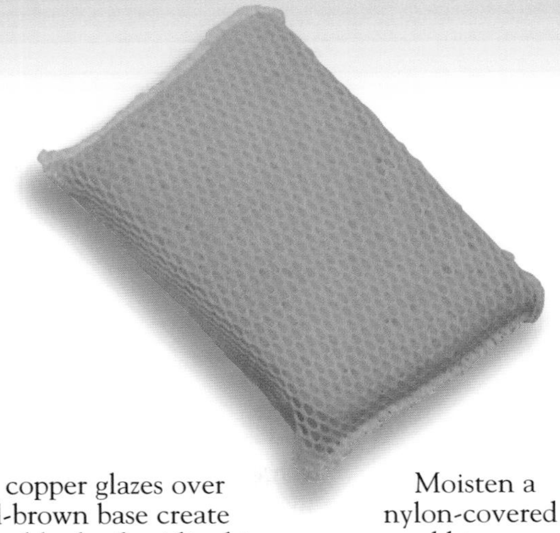

OXIDIZED IRON SUPPLIES

- Red-brown paint
- Copper acrylic paint
- Orange acrylic paint
- Water-base neutral glaze
- Scrubbing sponge with nylon-mesh cover
- 2-inch foam brush

Orange and copper glazes over a deep red-brown base create the rusty red look of oxidized iron. The orange glaze, showing the grid pattern of the nylon mesh covering on a scrubbing sponge, represents the etched texture of corroded iron. Here's how to paint the finish:

PROCEDURE: Cover the surface with one or two coats of red-brown paint in a satin or eggshell finish. Allow the base coat to dry thoroughly before applying the colored glaze.

Mix the copper- and orange-color glazes. Make a 50-50 mix of acrylic paint and neutral water-base glaze for each color. (You can also use oil-base paint and neutral glaze.) Mixing more neutral glaze than paint will make a more translucent glaze, lightening the effect.

Moisten a nylon-covered scrubbing sponge (shown above) to soften it. Then, with a 2-inch foam brush, spread a thin layer of copper glaze onto a separate flat disposable plate or a piece of cardboard. While the glaze is still wet, pat the scrubbing sponge into it to pick some up. Then pat the sponge onto the project surface. This will give the glaze a soft texture. Repeat this procedure until the whole surface has been treated. Don't overwork the surface; the more you pat the glazes, the less the texture will show from the nylon mesh covering the sponge.

Apply the orange glaze the same way, but apply it sparsely over the surface. You should be able to see the sponge's mesh texture clearly in the orange glaze. A thick glaze that adds some dimension to the surface heightens the effect. Turn the sponge as you work to create a random pattern.

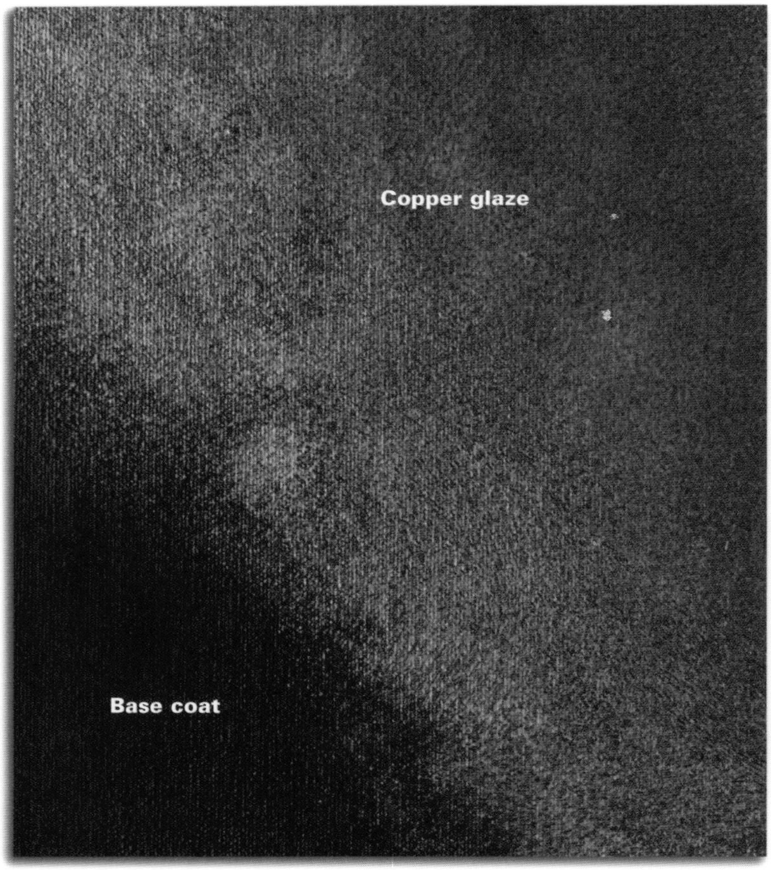

The mesh covering on the scrubbing sponge imparts texture to the oxidized iron finish.

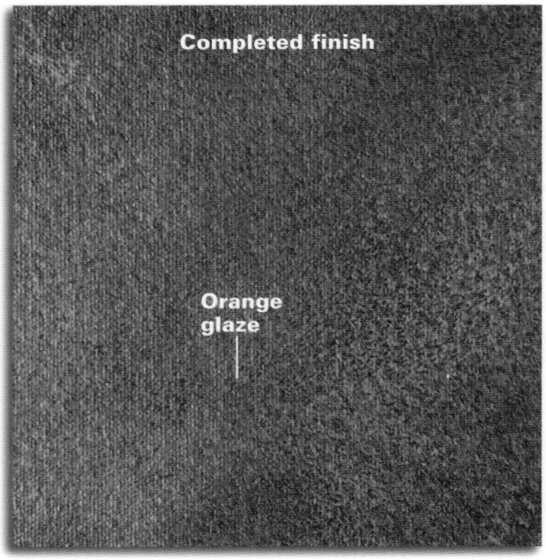

GLOSSARY

A

ACRYLIC: A synthetic resin used as the binder in high-quality latex paint. Acrylic paints are durable and resist fading.
ADHESION: The ability of a paint to stick to the underlying surface without lifting, peeling, cracking, or flaking.
ALKYD: A synthetic resin used as a vehicle or solvent for oil-base paints.
ANILINE DYE: A synthetic dye often used as a wood stain. Comes as a powder which is mixed with water, alcohol, or oil, depending on the dye.

B

BINDER: The agent in a paint that adheres the pigment to the surface and imparts a particular sheen to the finish.
BITE: The ability of a paint to adhere to a surface.
BLUE MASKING TAPE: A paint masking tape that can be removed from a surface without leaving residue or damaging the surface. Pressure along the edge can seal the tape to the surface to keep paint from creeping under it. See also *masking* and *masking tape*.
BRUSH SPINNER: A mechanical device that spins a paintbrush at high speed to remove thinners after cleaning. Can also be used for roller covers.

C

CEILING PAINT: A thick, flat, high-hiding paint made especially for ceilings. It can be tinted.
CELLULOSE SPONGE: A sponge made of synthetic material, usually with a regular shape. See *sea sponge*.
CHAIR RAIL: A decorative molding applied to a wall about 32 to 36 inches above the floor.
CHALK LINE: A straight line marked by snapping a chalk-covered string against a surface; also, the string used for marking a line in this way.
COLOR WASH: A decorative finish created by applying a tinted glaze over a base coat.
CRACKLE MEDIUM: Applied under or between coats of paint, crackle medium causes the paint to crack to simulate aging.
CRAZE: To make small cracks in a surface or a coat of finish.
CUTTING IN: Applying a narrow band of paint in corners of walls and ceilings and along trim.

D

DEAD CORNER: An inconspicuous corner in a room.
DEGLOSSING: Roughing up the surface of a coat of paint to promote better adhesion of new paint. Deglossing can be mechanical (as in sanding) or chemical.

E

EGGSHELL: A soft paint sheen, named for its likeness to the surface of a fresh eggshell. Sometimes called satin or low-luster.
ENAMEL: A paint with high binder content that dries to a hard, smooth finish. Enamel usually has a gloss or semigloss sheen.

F

FLAGGING: Split ends on paintbrush bristles that help the brush hold more paint and apply it more evenly.
FLAT: A nonreflective paint sheen. Sometimes called matte.
FRIEZE: A decorative border applied along the top of a wall, often stenciled.

G–H

GESSO: An opaque, white coating used to prepare a surface for painting.
GLAZE: A thin, transparent paint used for decorative effects.
GLAZE MEDIUM: A neutral-color translucent base that can be mixed with paint or artist's colors to make a glaze. Glaze medium is available in oil- or water-base.
GLOSS: A shiny paint sheen. Paint with a gloss sheen is usually enamel.
HIDING: A paint's ability to cover a previous coat of paint and prevent it from showing through. Also referred to as opacity.

L–O

LAP MARK: A visible overlap in paint. Can be caused by too much paint in the brush or roller or by painting over a dried edge.
LATEX: Water-base paint employing acrylic or vinyl resin or a blend of them as a binder.
LEVEL: Perfectly horizontal; parallel with the horizon. Also a tool for gauging level.
LEVELING: The ability of a paint to flow out smoothly on a surface so brush or roller marks don't show after the paint dries.
LUSTER: See *sheen*.
MASKING: Protecting an area or surface that isn't to be painted by covering it with tape or other material.

GLOSSARY
continued

MASKING TAPE: A low-tack, crepe-backed tape made for paint masking. Ordinary beige masking tape left on a surface too long can leave residue. See *blue masking tape*.
MATTE: Flat sheen.
MINERAL SPIRITS: Petroleum-base thinner for oil-base paints.
MURIATIC ACID: A dilute hydrochloric acid used for cleaning masonry. It is a hazardous material.
OIL-BASE: A paint or other finish in which an alkyd resin is the vehicle. Tools used with oil-base materials can be cleaned with a solvent. See *water-base*.
OIL PAINT: Artist's paint in which the vehicle is an oil. Usually a thick formulation, packaged in tubes.

P

PAINTER'S TAPE: Blue masking tape.
PAINTING TAPE: Masking tape with a microbarrier edge to keep paint from seeping through or creeping under.
PIGMENT: The finely ground color materials that give paint its color.
PLUMB: A true vertical line that is best found with a plumb bob.
PLUMB BOB: A weight that is attached to a string or chalk line. When hanging free, it shows a true vertical line.
POUNCE: To make short, sharp, up-and-down motions with a paintbrush or applicator.
PRIMER: A base coat applied to help paint adhere to a surface. Latex or oil-base primers are available. Specialty primers are sold for use over metal and in other special situations.

R

RESIN: A soluble substance that cures to a hard surface, used as a binder in paints. Most paint resins today are synthetic plastic materials, such as acrylic, vinyl, and urethane.
RESIST: To prevent paint from adhering to an area through the use of wax or some other material that paint won't stick to.

S

SATIN: A low-luster sheen.
SCRUBBABILITY: A paint's ability to stand up to repeated washing without fading or losing film thickness.
SEA SPONGE: A natural sponge from aquatic animals, usually irregular in shape. See *cellulose sponge*.
SEALER: An undercoat applied over porous or problem surfaces before painting. Sealer is sometimes called underbody.
SEMIGLOSS: A slightly reflective sheen.
SHEEN: The degree of light reflectivity of a painted surface. Also called luster or shine.
SHELLAC: A clear finish made by dissolving shellac flakes in alcohol. Used as a top coat and a sealer. As a sealer, shellac forms a strong barrier to keep stains from showing through a new finish.
SHINE: See *sheen*.
SOLVENT: The liquid used to thin paint or clean painting tools. Water is the solvent for latex paints; turpentine, paint thinner, or mineral spirits are solvents for oil-base paints. Also, the liquid component of paint.
SPACKLING COMPOUND: A paste for filling cracks, holes, and dents in wallboard, plaster, or painted woodwork.
STAIN: A transparent colorant for wood. Stains may be pigmented (like thinned paint) or dye stains.

T

TEXTURED PAINT: Thick paint, often containing granular material, that imparts texture to a surface.
THINNER: A liquid used to reduce the consistency of a paint for brushing, rolling, or spraying. See also *solvent*.
TOOTH: A surface coarseness that improves the adherence of paint.
TSP: Trisodium phosphate, a cleaning and deglossing agent; mix ¼ cup per gallon of water.
TURPENTINE: A thinner for oil-base paints derived from natural pine resins.

U-W

UNDERBODY: See *sealer*.
UNIFORMITY: Even appearance of color and sheen on a surface.
VEHICLE: The base of a paint. See *solvent*.
VINYL: A synthetic resin used as a binder in latex paints.
WAINSCOT: The lower part of wall when it has a different covering or finish than the upper part.
WASHABLE: Paint or wallcovering that can be cleaned with a mild detergent, water, and a sponge or rag.
WATER-BASE: A paint or other finish in which water is the vehicle. Tools used with water-base materials can be cleaned with soap and water. See *oil-base*.
WET EDGE: The undried edge of a painting stroke that helps blend the stroke into the adjacent one.
WET ON WET: A method of applying paint over a wet base coat to promote blending.

INDEX

METRIC CONVERSIONS

U.S. Units to Metric Equivalents

To Convert From	Multiply By	To Get
Inches	25.4	Millimeters
Inches	2.54	Centimeters
Feet	30.48	Centimeters
Feet	0.3048	Meters
Yards	0.9144	Meters
Square inches	6.4516	Square centimeters
Square feet	0.0929	Square meters
Square yards	0.8361	Square meters
Acres	0.4047	Hectares
Cubic inches	16.387	Cubic centimeters
Cubic feet	0.0283	Cubic meters
Cubic feet	28.316	Liters
Cubic yards	0.7646	Cubic meters
Cubic yards	764.55	Liters

To convert from degrees Fahrenheit (F) to degrees Celsius (C), first subtract 32, then multiply by $\frac{5}{9}$.

Metric Units to U.S. Equivalents

To Convert From	Multiply By	To Get
Millimeters	0.0394	Inches
Centimeters	0.3937	Inches
Centimeters	0.0328	Feet
Meters	3.2808	Feet
Meters	1.0936	Yards
Square centimeters	0.1550	Square inches
Square meters	10.764	Square feet
Square meters	1.1960	Square yards
Hectares	2.4711	Acres
Cubic centimeters	0.0610	Cubic inches
Cubic meters	35.315	Cubic feet
Liters	0.0353	Cubic feet
Cubic meters	1.308	Cubic yards
Liters	0.0013	Cubic yards

To convert from degrees Celsius to degrees Fahrenheit, multiply by $\frac{9}{5}$, then add 32.